OECD Tax Policy Reviews: Costa Rica 2017

BETTER POLICIES FOR BETTER LIVES

The *OECD Tax Policy Reviews: Costa Rica 2017* report has been prepared by the OECD Secretariat on the basis of currently available information as at 1 April 2017 and does not prejudge in any way the results of the ongoing reviews of Costa Rica by OECD committees as part of the process of accession to the OECD.

Please cite this publication as:
OECD (2017), *OECD Tax Policy Reviews: Costa Rica 2017*, OECD Publishing, Paris.
http://dx.doi.org/10.1787/9789264277724-en

ISBN 978-92-64-27770-0 (print)
ISBN 978-92-64-27772-4 (PDF)

Photo credits: Cover © mbrand85/shutterstock.com.

Corrigenda to OECD publications may be found on line at: *www.oecd.org/about/publishing/corrigenda.htm*.

Foreword

This report provides a comprehensive tax policy assessment of Costa Rica's current tax system as well as tax policy reform recommendations. The report is divided into five chapters, starting with a general chapter providing an overview of key macroeconomic and tax revenue trends (Chapter 1), followed by an assessment of the main types of taxes of the Costa Rican tax system, including corporate income taxes (Chapter 2), personal income taxes and social security contributions (Chapter 3), the general sales tax (Chapter 4) and environmentally-related taxes (Chapter 5).

This report is part of a new series of publications entitled *OECD Tax Policy Reviews*. OECD Tax Policy Reviews are intended to provide independent, comprehensive and comparative assessments of OECD member and non-member countries' tax systems as well as concrete recommendations for tax policy reform. By benchmarking countries' tax systems and identifying tailored tax policy reform options, the ultimate objective of the *Reviews* is to enhance the design of existing tax policies and to support the adoption and implementation of tax policy reforms.

This report was written by Bert Brys, Sarah Perret, Sarita Gómez, Johanna Arlinghaus and Tibor Hanappi and led by Bert Brys and Sarah Perret. The analysis is primarily based on desk research, OECD statistics and tax modelling tools as well as the findings from a fact-finding mission which took place in San José in the second week of October in 2016. The authors of the report would like to thank Costa Rica's *Ministerio de Hacienda* for their assistance in organising the mission and for follow-up support in the drafting stage of the review. Thank you also to COMEX (*Ministerio de Comercio Exterior Costa Rica*) and to the Ministry of Environment from Costa Rica for their comments. The authors are also grateful to Sonia Araujo, Piet Battiau, Juan Carlos Benitez Molina, Nils Axel Braathen, David Bradbury, Stéphane Buydens, Jeremiah Coder, Nathalie Girouard, Mark Johnson, Dimitra Koulouri, Horacio Levy, Patrick Lenain, Giorgia Maffini, Angel Melguizo, Sebastian Nieto Parra and Kurt Van Dender from the OECD Secretariat for useful comments and suggestions.

Table of contents

Figures

Tables

Boxes

Executive summary

Costa Rica faces major tax policy challenges

Costa Rica's tax revenues are close to the Latin American and Caribbean (LAC) average but, notwithstanding recent efforts to reduce expenditure, they are insufficient to finance the country's current spending needs. Higher tax revenues should primarily come from broadening tax bases as well as from enhanced efforts to tackle tax avoidance and evasion and to bring in more informal taxpayers within the formal economy.

In addition to raising more tax revenues to balance its budget, Costa Rica needs to address the distortive nature of its tax mix and enhance the redistributive role of its tax system. In particular, Costa Rica should, once a balanced budget has been achieved, shift taxation away from social security contributions (SSCs), which weigh heavily on formal employment, towards less economically distortive taxes including the value added tax (VAT) and environmentally-related taxes. In addition, the role of the personal income tax (PIT) should be strengthened as it currently raises little revenue and does not contribute to reducing inequality.

The excessive earmarking of tax revenues, which strongly constrains the government's public finance decisions will need to be reformed if Costa Rica is to place itself on a path of fiscal sustainability in the long run.

Reforming the corporate tax system

Costa Rica levies a relatively high corporate income tax (CIT) rate on a narrow tax base. Businesses face a tax-induced incentive to finance investment with debt rather than with newly issued equity. Foreign-source passive income is not taxed, which is uncommon. Businesses face relatively high effective tax rates (ETRs) which discourage foreign direct investment (FDI). A wide-range of CIT incentives are in place such as for companies in Free Trade Zones (FTZs). The FTZ tax regime lowers the tax burden significantly for investment from countries with a territorial tax system but not for countries with a worldwide tax system; for those investments, the FTZ regime implies a tax revenue transfer from Costa Rica to the investing country. Costa Rica should regularly undertake a comprehensive cost-benefit analysis of all of its various corporate tax incentives, including its FTZ regime, to assess their net benefits in terms of additional investment, employment and productivity and to evaluate how the design of those tax incentives could be improved.

Strengthening the role of the personal income tax

Social security contributions (SSCs) weigh heavily on formal employment while only few people are subject to PIT. The lack of integration between the PIT and SSC administrations lies at the heart of Costa Rica's labour market challenges. Because social security funds generally have to finance their own expenditure, they end up levying high SSCs. This results in high average tax burdens on labour income and labour costs, thereby reducing formal work incentives and employers' formal labour demand. The limited revenues from PIT also imply that labour taxes do not play a significant role in redistributing income. Collecting greater revenues from PIT, by lowering the income threshold above which PIT has to be paid as well as by introducing additional PIT brackets and gradually raising the top PIT rate, could contribute to reducing income inequality. Costa Rica should aim at better integrating the tax and social security systems, including through improved information sharing between the tax and SSC administrations, and harmonising the tax treatment of different types of labour income to reduce distortions and tax avoidance opportunities.

Putting in place a modern VAT system

Costa Rica does not have a modern VAT system in place. The current general sales tax exempts services except for those that are explicitly included in the law. In addition to reducing the tax's neutrality, this narrow tax base generates a significant loss in potential revenues. The sales tax system is also somewhat regressive, due to the existence of exemptions that primarily benefit richer households. Costa Rica's priority should be to introduce a well-designed and broad-based VAT system, covering both goods and services, to be able to generate additional revenues and remove existing distortions. Additional reforms, notably related to the way VAT credits are granted and to the taxation of cross-border supplies of services, will also be needed to enhance the tax's neutrality.

Using tax policy to address selected environmental challenges

There is scope to improve the environmental effectiveness of tax policy while also increasing revenues. In particular, the excise tax on fuels could be extended to cover all fossil fuels and rates could be aligned better with external costs. Since they create a *de facto* preferential treatment for fuels, the sales and import tax exemptions for fuels should be reconsidered. In addition, vehicle tax design can be adapted to better align with achieving environmental policy objectives such as curbing air pollution and congestion. To level the playing field, the tax treatment of public and private electricity producers could be harmonised. The cost-effectiveness of the Payments for Environmental Services Programme in providing environmental benefits has to be evaluated.

Key recommendations

- Raise more tax revenues to balance the budget.
- Move away from the excessive earmarking of tax revenues.
- Gradually rebalance the tax mix away from SSCs towards VAT, income taxes and environmentally-related taxes as the budget is returned to a balanced position.
- Convert the sales tax into a modern VAT with a broad base that includes services.

- Increase the standard VAT rate to help balance the budget.
- Strengthen the role of the tax and transfer systems in lowering inequality by broadening the PIT base and raising top PIT rates.
- Better integrate the PIT and SSCs administrations, in particular through enhanced exchange of information.
- Reduce exemptions for environmentally related taxes and align tax rates more closely with external costs.
- Broaden the CIT base by taxing foreign-source passive income, introducing a profit-based interest limitation rule, and evaluate the design of the wide range of corporate tax incentives. Over time, the standard CIT rate should be gradually lowered.
- Address tax avoidance and evasion by reinforcing the tax administration, harmonising the tax treatment of different types of income, and strengthening international tax rules.

Chapter 1

Overview of Costa Rica's fiscal and tax policy challenges

This chapter discusses the level and composition of the tax revenue raised by Costa Rica. The chapter focuses on key macro-level indicators of the Costa Rican economy, including the country's level of economic growth, the unemployment rate, the level of inequality, the budget deficit and the country's debt level. Specific institutional design characteristics are discussed, including the earmarking of tax revenues. The chapter focuses on the level of tax avoidance and evasion in the country. The chapter also lists the country's tax reform plans. This chapter sets the scene for the in-depth tax policy discussion in the rest of the report.

Despite significant economic and social progress, Costa Rica faces major challenges

Costa Rica has made significant economic and social progress. Real GDP per capita has been increasing (Figure 1.1), nearly doubling over the past 30 years. GDP per capita was less than half of the OECD average in 2015 and remains below the values which can be found in some of the best performing Latin-America and the Caribbean (LAC) countries (Figure 1.2). However, real GDP per capita continues to increase at rates which outperform many other LAC and most OECD countries. Moreover, partly thanks to virtually universal health care, pension and primary education systems, Costa Rica ranks well on broad socio-economic and well-being indicators (OECD, 2016a).

Figure 1.1. **Percentage change in GDP per capita, Costa Rica, LAC and OECD**

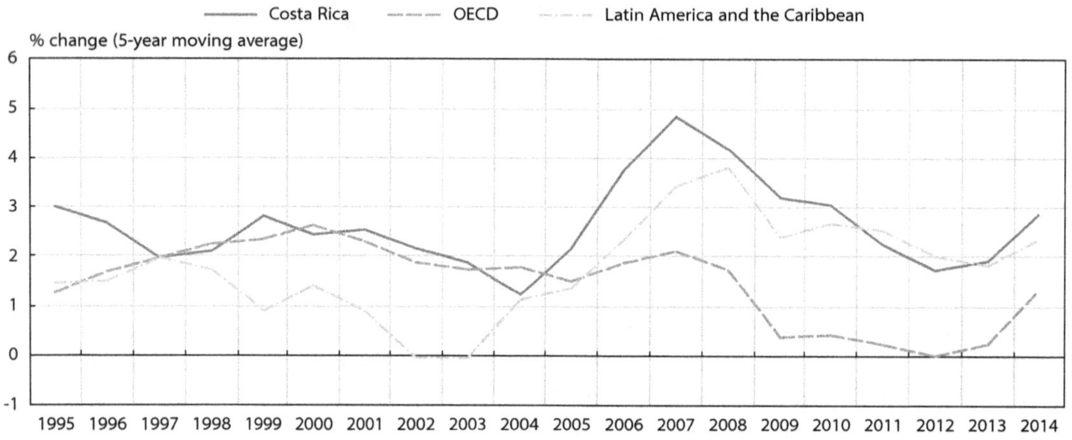

StatLink http://dx.doi.org/10.1787/888933544398

Note: Annual growth of GDP per capita in PPP, constant 2011 international USD (5-year moving average).

Source: OECD Economic Surveys. Costa Rica Economic Assessment, 2016.

Figure 1.2. **GDP per capita in PPP (current international USD)**

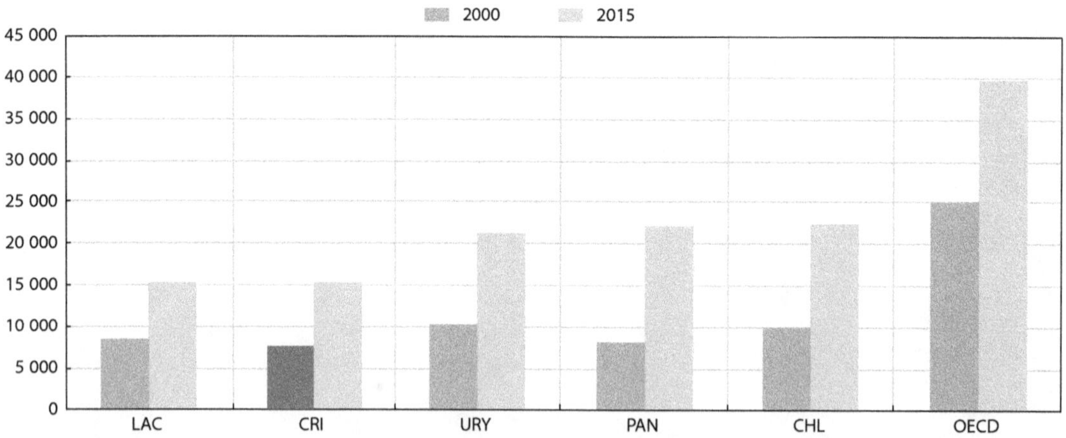

StatLink http://dx.doi.org/10.1787/888933544417

Source: World Development Indicators.

Progress has also been achieved in the area of environmental protection. Costa Rica is the only country in the region, and in fact one of the few countries worldwide, which has reversed deforestation. The country is also a pioneer in the development of eco-tourism with a positive impact on the income of local workers (OECD, 2016a).

The process of opening up to international trade and investment which started in the early 1980s has diversified the country's production structure, boosted exports and labour force utilisation (OECD, 2016a). Foreign direct investment (FDI) by multinational enterprises (MNEs) contributed to the transitioning of the economy from a rural and agricultural based economy to one with high value-added industries (The World Bank Group, 2015).

The United States is by far the largest investor country in Costa Rica. Table 1.1 shows data on bilateral FDI stocks and net inflows from the most important investor countries, including the largest Latin American economies as well as other countries with FDI stocks at or above 190 million USD in 2012. FDI stocks from Spain have almost doubled in the two years after the tax treaty with Costa Rica became effective in 2011, making it the second largest investor country in 2012. Considerable FDI stocks are also held by investors from Mexico and Great Britain although FDI inflows from these countries have netted out in recent years.

Table 1.1. **FDI stocks and flows in Costa Rica by investor country (in million USD)**

	FDI Stocks				Net FDI Inflows			
	2009	2010	2011	2012	2009	2010	2011	2012
Belgium	217	220	231	247	12	0	0	12
Canada	171	223	261	273	17	12	9	-10
Germany	174	198	198	190	10	-2	59	118
Italy	51	50	113	233	27	14	30	32
Netherlands	242	253	281	318	79	28	247	318
Spain	734	775	1 025	1 359	27	20	-30	12
Switzerland	382	457	476	482	-32	68	5	-3
UK	877	906	877	902	33	49	42	8
US	7 885	9 050	10 347	11 513	1 022	1 031	1 376	1 051
Argentina	16	16	14	22	8	0	0	8
Brazil	17	12	26	119	-5	-6	8	92
Chile	14	17	18	13	3	2	2	-6
Colombia	127	230	363	481	6	101	152	112
Mexico	416	464	616	973	0	0	0	0
Peru	2	5	8	14	9	15	34	142
Venezuela	171	189	209	356	7	40	183	346

Source: UNCTAD.

However, a number of economic vulnerabilities have emerged. While export-oriented firms are dynamic and innovative due to inward FDI and well-developed links with global value chains, domestic firms are still concentrated on low value-added activities and often operate in the informal economy, which accounts for around 40% of total employment

(OECD, 2016a). Since the financial crisis, Costa Rica has also experienced rapidly-increasing public deficits and debt. As a result of those vulnerabilities, Moody's Investors Services downgraded Costa Rica's credit rating in February 2016 to Ba1, and again in February 2017 to a speculative grade Ba2.

A challenging reform agenda lies ahead to overcome the middle-income trap. Despite its favourable performance in terms of GDP per capita growth in the past decade, Costa Rica has remained as an upper-middle income country since 2000, highlighting the need to increase productivity growth to overcome the so-called middle-income trap. Similar to other emerging economies, arriving at middle-income levels usually requires new engines of economic growth, which are based on capital- and skill-intensive manufacturing and service industries (OECD/ECLAC/CAF, 2016). Similar to other Latin American economies, and following the experiences of countries that have moved from middle-income to high-income countries, Costa Rica needs to adopt a comprehensive agenda that encompasses a wide range of policy areas, including raising more tax revenues, improving the quality of education and strengthening the access to financial markets (Melguizo et al., 2017).

Costa Rica is also facing inclusiveness challenges. Unemployment has been rising since 2007 and is now close to 10%, above both OECD and LAC average levels (Figure 1.3). Costa Rica's economy is characterised by the presence of a large informal sector. Informality rates for adults (35-64 years old) increased between 2004 and 2014 from 23.8% to 25.8% while in the LAC region on average they decreased from 47% to 38.3% over the same period (OECD/ECLAC/CAF, 2016). High informality impacts those on both low and middle incomes as the lack of formal jobs increases the probability that losing a formal job implies falling into poverty (OECD/ECLAC/CAF, 2016). In addition, while Costa Rica stands out among LAC countries in several social dimensions, inequality has been increasing since the mid-1990s to high levels by OECD standards. The rise in inequality is also in stark contrast with many other Latin American economies (Figure 1.4), which have made significant progress in reducing simultaneously inequality and poverty (OECD, 2016a).

Figure 1.3. **Unemployment rates, international comparison**

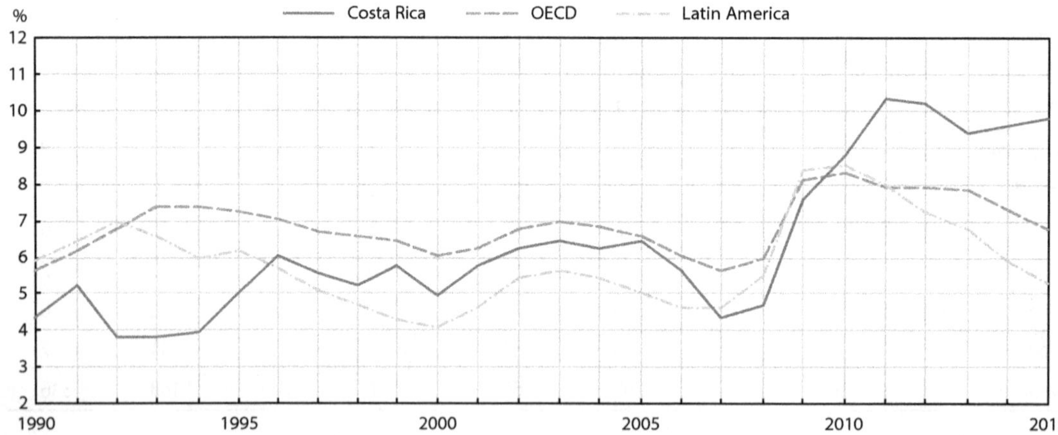

StatLink http://dx.doi.org/10.1787/888933544436

Source: OECD Economic Surveys. Costa Rica Economic Assessment, 2016.

Figure 1.4. **Evolution of inequality in Costa Rica and LAC countries**

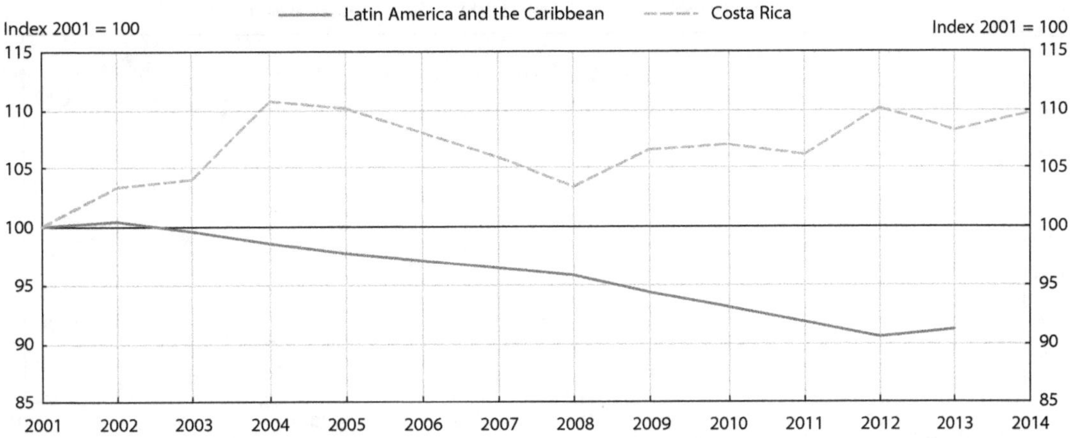

StatLink http://dx.doi.org/10.1787/888933544455

Source: OECD Economic Surveys. Costa Rica Economic Assessment, 2016.

Budget deficits and public debt have been rising to unsustainable levels

High deficits have resulted in a rapidly increasing public debt which is increasingly difficult to service given current tax revenues. Costa Rica's central government budget went from a surplus 0.57% of GDP in 2007 to a deficit of 5.2% of GDP in recent years (Figure 1.5) (Ministerio de Hacienda, 2017). Public debt rose from about 25% of GDP in 2008 to more than 40% in 2015 (OECD, 2016a) (Figure 1.6). The level of public debt in Costa Rica is high compared to the estimated average public debt level in LAC countries, which was about 36% of GDP in 2015 (ECLAC, 2016). Moreover, debt levels as a share of government revenues in Costa Rica are unsustainably high and have increased more than in any other country in the region. From 2010 to 2015, the ratio increased by 84 percentage points (Figure 1.7). In Brazil, which experienced the second largest increase in debt as a percentage of government revenues, the increase was around 52 percentage points. The debt level in 2015 was almost three times as high as total annual government revenue, which puts Costa Rica in the top, after El Salvador.

Figure 1.5. **Budget balance as a percentage of GDP**

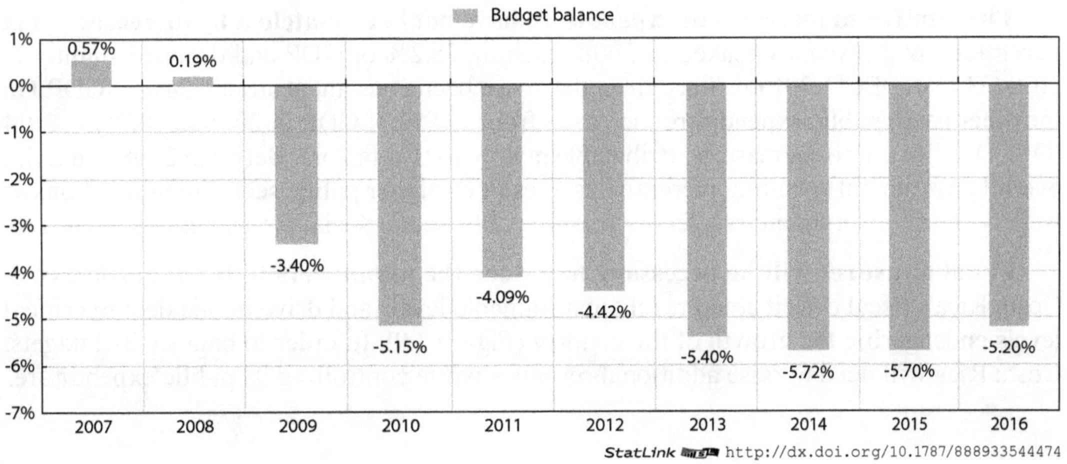

StatLink http://dx.doi.org/10.1787/888933544474

Source: Finance Ministry Costa Rica, 2017.

Figure 1.6. **Public debt as a percentage of GDP**

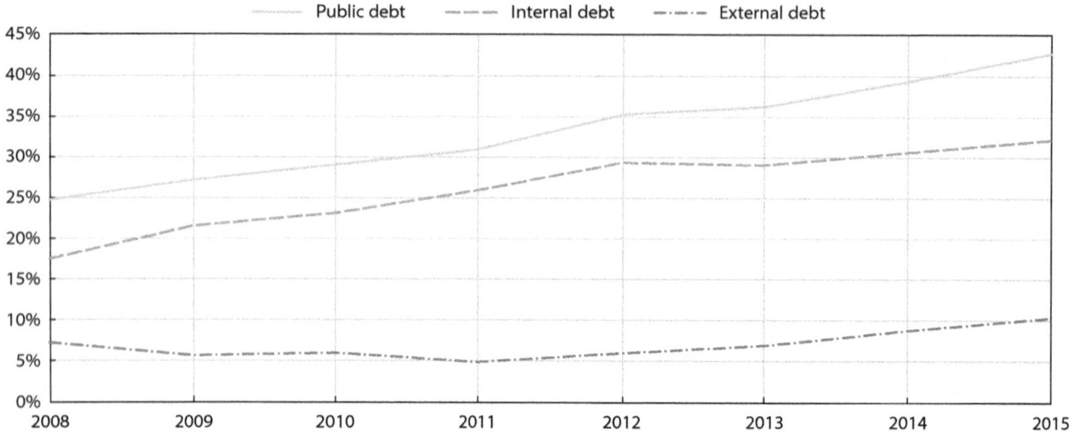

StatLink http://dx.doi.org/10.1787/888933544493

Source: Ministerio de Hacienda, 2017.

Figure 1.7. **Public debt as a % of government revenues – Costa Rica and LAC countries**

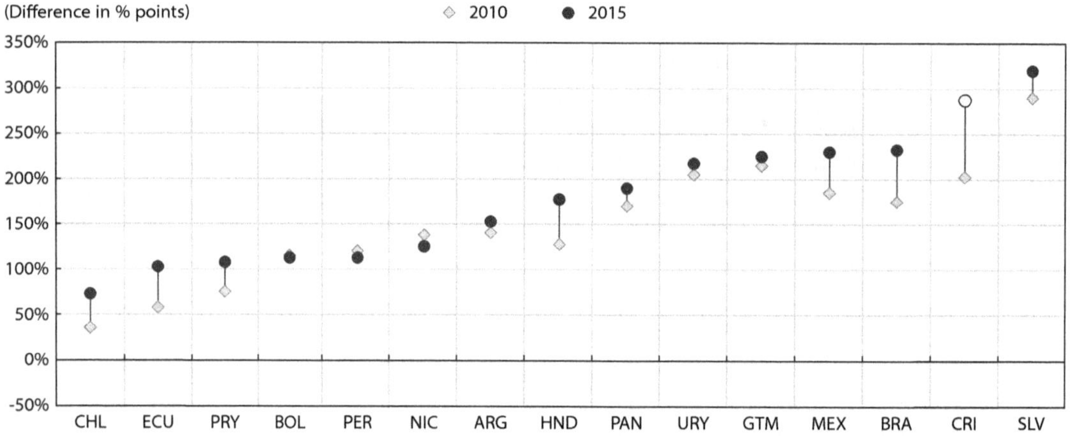

StatLink http://dx.doi.org/10.1787/888933544512

Source: Adelfang, "Tenemos las peores finanzas pública de Latinoamérica?", at La República, 2016.

The significant increases in expenditure have not been matched by increases in tax revenues. Total revenues peaked in 2008 reaching 25.2% of GDP and dropped slightly in 2010 (23.7%) (OECD, 2016b). Since then, they have been constant at around 24% of GDP. On the other hand, public expenditure increased from 23.9% of GDP in 2008 to 30.7% in 2014 (OECD, 2016a). This increase is attributable mainly to two factors. Between 2008 and 2013, overall government spending increased as a result of higher public sector remunerations as well as higher government transfers to finance public sector social programmes (Figure 1.8).

Fiscal measures will be necessary to reduce the public deficit. If left unaddressed, Costa Rica's fiscal deficit could reach unsustainable levels and drive public debt to critical levels endangering the growth of the country (Figure 1.9). In order to balance its budgets, Costa Rica will need to raise additional revenues while controlling its public expenditure.

Figure 1.8. **Composition of expenditure (% of GDP at market prices)**

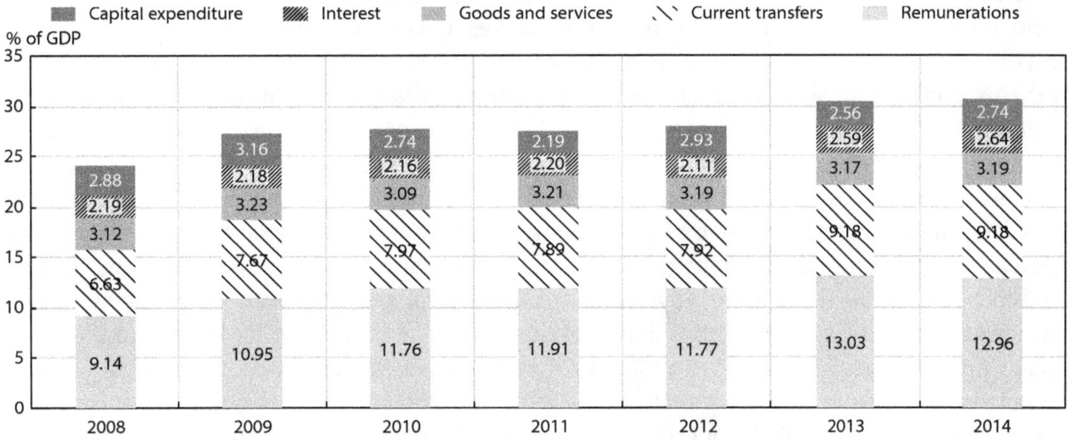

StatLink http://dx.doi.org/10.1787/888933544531

Source: OECD Economic Surveys. Costa Rica Economic Assessment, 2016.

Figure 1.9. **Government debt as a % of GDP**

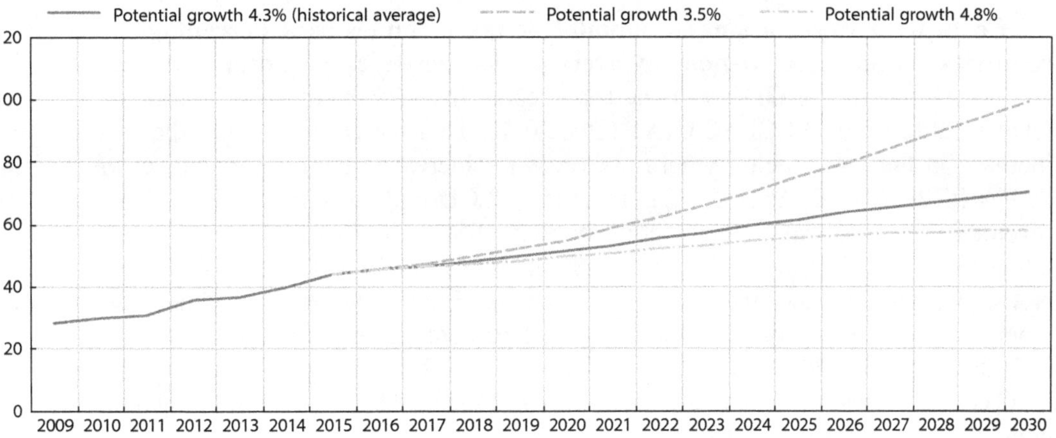

StatLink http://dx.doi.org/10.1787/888933544550

Note: All estimations assume a fiscal multiplier of 0.3 (IMF, 2015), and an expenditure growing at the same pace as nominal GDP.

Source: OECD Economic Surveys. Costa Rica Economic Assessment, 2016.

Earmarking of tax revenues has become dis-functional

Earmarking of tax revenues in Costa Rica strongly limits government's discretionary power. Costa Rica guarantees the funding of most public programmes and institutions through the earmarking of tax revenues; a fixed percentage of tax revenues is pre-set and the corresponding revenues go to finance those programmes and institutions. For instance, 8% of total tax revenues is allocated to the Ministry of Education and 6% of tax revenues is paid to the judicial branch. In 2014, for example, around 70% of central government expenditure was mandated by constitutional and other legal provisions; net of interest payments, this leaves only about 17% of the central government's budget to be used for discretionary spending measures (OECD, 2016a).

Although earmarking of tax revenues guarantees a consistent funding of government expenditure, it leads to distortions in the allocation of public funds, to over- and under-funding of government programmes and makes it very costly to balance the budget. In countries which face governance challenges, a certain degree of earmarking of revenues may guarantee a stable source of funding over time of key expenditure items, such as the education system. Earmarking may also raise transparency and taxpayers' trust in government and ultimately encourage greater tax compliance. However, it constrains the flexibility that governments have in the management of public funds. Any increase in tax revenues translates into increasing transfers to earmarked programmes irrespective of whether they need additional funding and there are no procedures in place for entities with an excess budget to make refunds to the central government. Earmarking can thus lead to overspending on earmarked objectives. On the other hand, earmarking can lead to the under-funding of other social programmes and public investment if funds have already been earmarked to other objectives. Finally, earmarking makes balancing the budget more difficult; i.e. in order to service a budget deficit of 5% of GDP, tax revenues will need to raise significantly more given that part of the additional revenues will automatically be allocated to earmarked objectives.

Total level of tax revenues is similar to the LAC average but the tax mix differs significantly

Costa Rica raises a similar amount of tax revenues as a percentage of GDP to countries in the LAC region on average. Tax revenues in Costa Rica increased by 3 percentage points of GDP over the last decade; from 20.1% of GDP in 2006 to 23.1% of GDP in 2015 (OECD/ECLAC/CIAT/IDB, 2017). This increase is higher than the average increase in the LAC region where tax revenues increased by 1.9 percentage points from 20.9% in 2006 to 22.8% of GDP in 2015 (OECD/ECLAC/CIAT/IDB, 2017). Total tax revenues net of social security contributions (SSCs) in Costa Rica increased by only 0.6 percentage points of GDP: from 14.7% of GDP in 2006 to 15.3% of GDP in 2015. This is a significantly smaller increase than on average in the LAC region (without Costa Rica), where tax revenues net of SSCs increased by 1 percentage point of GDP from 18.1% of GDP in 2006 to 19.1% in 2015 (OECD/ECLAC/CIAT/IDB, 2017). Despite being slightly above the LAC countries' average, the tax-to-GDP ratio in Costa Rica remains low compared to OECD countries (Figures 1.10 and 1.11).

Figure 1.10. **Tax to GDP ratio, Costa Rica, OECD and LAC countries**

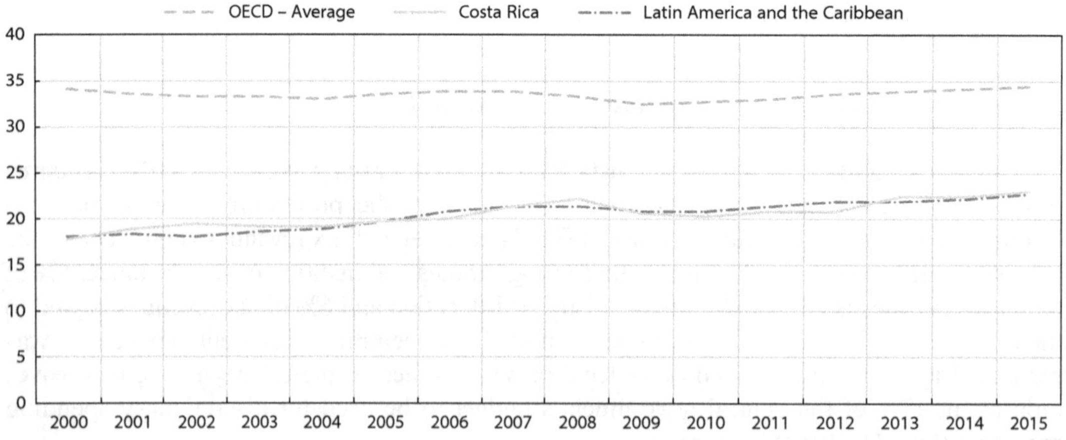

StatLink http://dx.doi.org/10.1787/888933544569

Source: OECD Global Revenue Statistics Database; OECD/ECLAC/CIAT/IDB (2017).

Figure 1.11. **Tax to GDP ratio in LAC region per country (2015)**

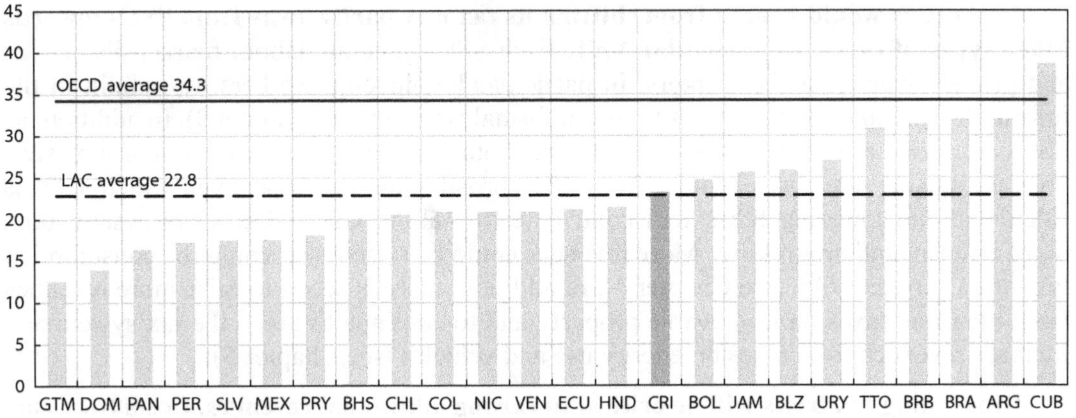

StatLink http://dx.doi.org/10.1787/888933544588

Source: OECD Global Revenue Statistics Database; OECD/ECLAC/CIAT/IDB (2017).

Costa Rica's tax mix is tilted towards SSCs. Costa Rica raises more revenue from SSCs and less revenue from income taxes compared to countries on average in the LAC region and the OECD (Figure 1.12). In 2014, SSCs accounted for 34% of total tax revenue in Costa Rica, while they accounted for about 15.9% of total revenues in LAC countries and 26.2% in the OECD. In addition, Costa Rica raises payroll taxes, which further increase the tax burden on labour income, while this category is a very minor source of revenues in the LAC region and the OECD on average. Taxes on goods and services including valued added tax (VAT) and environmentally related taxes accounted for 40.3% of Costa Rica's total tax revenues, which is below the share in the LAC region of about 49% of total tax revenues. Revenues from the personal income tax (PIT) and the corporate income tax (CIT) amounted to only 18.2% of total revenues, below the LAC average of 28.3% and far below the OECD average of 33.7%. Finally, property taxes accounted for only a very small share of total tax revenues at 1.9% of tax revenues, almost half of the average for LAC countries, and only one third of the OECD average.

Figure 1.12. **Tax mix as a % of total revenues (2014)**

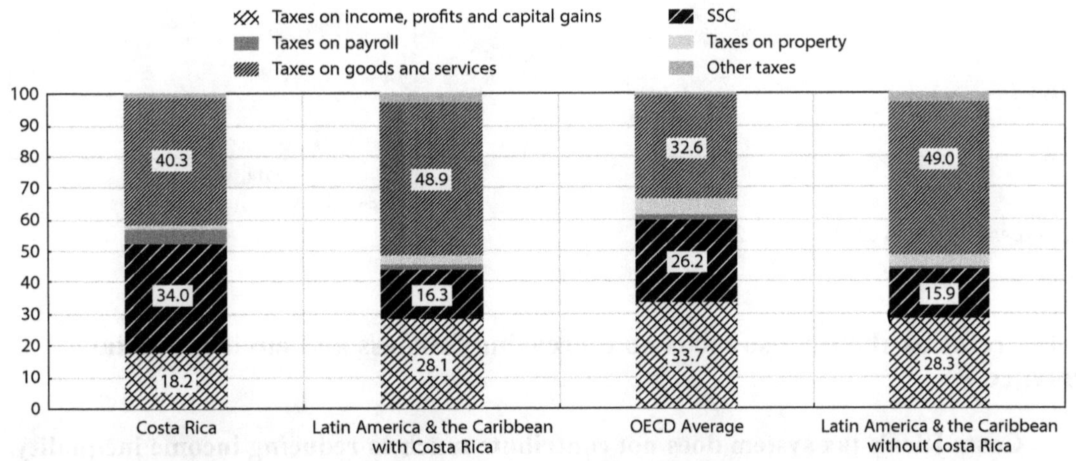

StatLink http://dx.doi.org/10.1787/888933544607

Source: OECD Global Revenue Statistics Database; OECD/ECLAC/CIAT/IDB (2017).

A structural tax reform would also rebalance the tax mix

Costa Rica would benefit from shifting its tax mix partly away from SSCs towards other types of taxes, in particular VAT. High SSCs generate labour market distortions and provide incentives for workers, in particular low-income workers, to remain in the informal sector and for employers to hire informal workers (see Chapter 3). In addition, as SSCs are levied at flat rates, they do not contribute to making the tax system progressive. Overall, raising greater revenues from PIT, broadening the base over which CIT is calculated and lowering SSCs will contribute to making Costa Rica's tax system both more efficient and progressive. More revenues could be raised by turning the consumption tax into a genuine VAT (see Chapter 4). In addition, there is scope to raise more revenues from recurrent taxes on immovable property and to continue to green the tax system and increase revenues from taxes on energy use and vehicles (see Chapter 5).

Broadening tax bases will be critical to raising additional revenues. Costa Rica's tax bases are narrow. The amount of tax expenditures in Costa Rica is very large and come at a large fiscal cost, particularly within the CIT, PIT and VAT. In 2014, total tax expenditure amounted to 5.1% of GDP: 2.9% for VAT, 1.9% for PIT and CIT and 0.3% for other taxes (Ministerio de Hacienda, 2014). These shares have been relatively stable since 2010 (Figure 1.13). In addition to their fiscal cost, tax expenditures generate distortions between different types of taxpayers, they make the tax system harder to administer, increase compliance costs, and they tend to make tax systems less equitable as better-off taxpayers often benefit more from them than poorer households.

Figure 1.13. **Tax expenditure as a % of GDP**

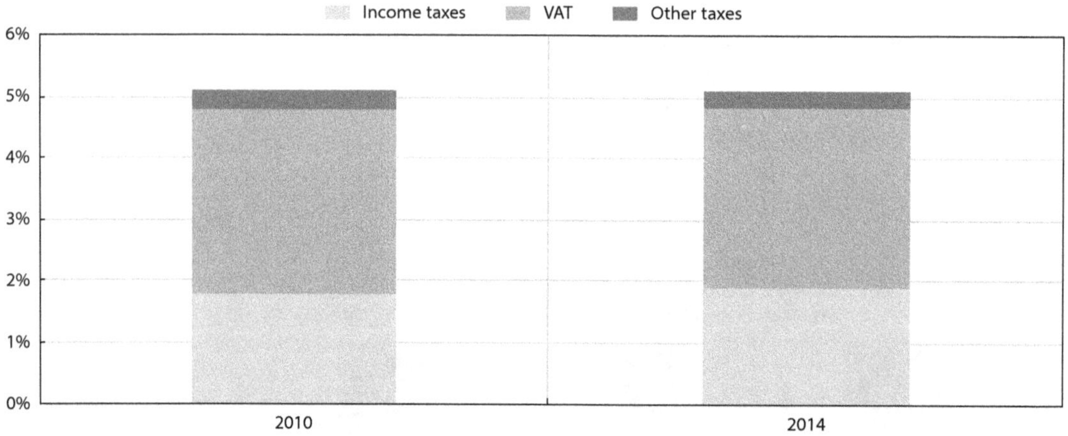

StatLink http://dx.doi.org/10.1787/888933544626

Source: Ministerio de Hacienda, 2014.

Future tax reforms should also focus on increasing fairness and environmental performance

Costa Rica's tax system does not contribute much to reducing income inequality. In general in OECD countries, taxes play an important role in redistribution and narrowing income gaps across the population. In Costa Rica, however, the tax system does not contribute much to redistributing income from richer to poorer households, as shown by the very small difference between the Gini coefficients before and after taxes and transfers (Figure 1.14). The fact that the PIT plays only a limited role in Costa Rica partly explains this result (Chapter 3).

Figure 1.14. **International comparison of inequality**

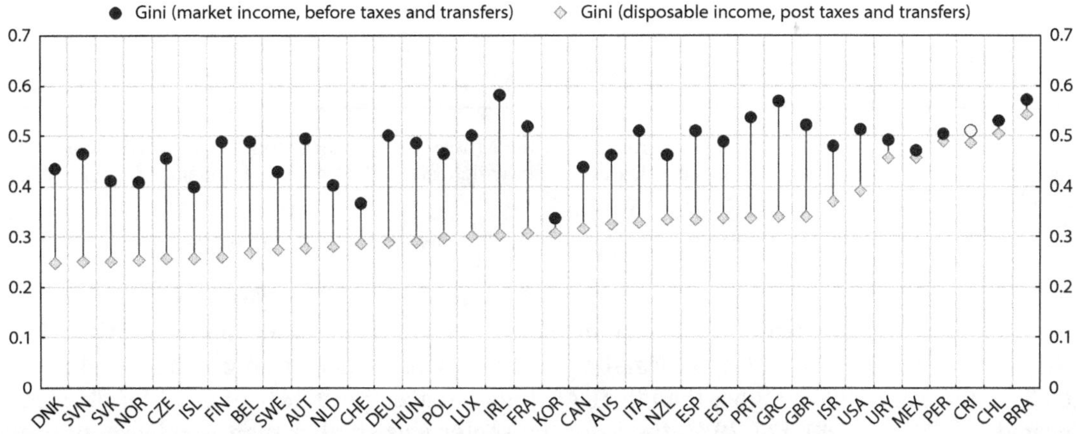

StatLink http://dx.doi.org/10.1787/888933544645

Source: OECD Economic Surveys. Costa Rica Economic Assessment, 2016.

The schedular nature of Costa Rica's tax system violates tax equity principles, ultimately reducing the tax system's equity. The tax system taxes different types of personal income differently; this is in particular the case for employment and personal business income (see Chapter 3). This violates the horizontal equity tax principle, as taxpayers earning the same amount of income but receiving it through different sources will be taxed differently, and it violates vertical equity as those on higher incomes do not necessarily pay higher taxes than those on lower incomes.

Finally, tax reforms could help Costa Rica reach its ambitious domestic environmental and climate policy targets in a cost-effective way. While, compared to other OECD countries, Costa Rica raises a relatively large share of revenues as a percentage of GDP from environmentally-related taxes, there is scope to improve the environmental effectiveness of tax policy while also increasing revenues. For example, the rates of the excise tax on fuels could be adjusted to better reflect the external cost associated with the use of these fuels, and the vehicle taxes can be reformed to better address air pollution and congestion. However, even beyond environmentally-related taxes, there is scope to align the tax policy framework with environmental and climate policy objectives. In particular, the sales and import tax exemptions that apply to products subject to the fuel tax translate into a de facto preferential treatment of fuels compared to other products, and could be reconsidered.

The efforts to fight against tax evasion have to be increased

Tax evasion in Costa Rica is widespread. Foregone tax revenues as a result of tax evasion are very high, in particular within the CIT (Table 1.2); a study by Bachas and Soto (2016) shows that Costa Rican corporations evade up to 70% of their CIT liability when they face the 30% statutory CIT rate. Non-compliance with the sales tax is also a critical issue (see Chapter 4). Given the very high fiscal deficits, addressing those high levels of tax avoidance and evasion is crucial and should be a key focus of any tax reform.

Table 1.2. **Tax avoidance and evasion estimates as a % of GDP**

	2010	2011	2012	2013
Total	8.21	7.98	7.82	8.22
Sales tax (including the effect of reduced rates)*	2.36	2.30	2.31	2.36
Income tax	5.85	5.68	5.51	5.86
Employees	*0.18*	*0.19*	*0.10*	*0.23*
Self-employed	*1.34*	*1.30*	*1.34*	*1.40*
Corporations	*4.33*	*4.18*	*4.06*	*4.23*

* The aggregate tax avoidance estimates (provided by the Ministry of Finance from Costa Rica) include the revenue foregone as a result of reduced sales tax rates, which the OECD does not consider as being "tax avoidance".

Source: Dirección General de Hacienda, Estadísticas Fiscales, División de Política Fiscal, 2015.

The high tax burden is a key driver of the informal economy in Costa Rica. The IMF estimated the size of the informal economy in Costa Rica at approximately 42% of GDP in the early 2000s, higher than the LAC regional average at 38% of GDP for the same period (Vuletin, 2008). For 2012, the informal sector was smaller than in other countries in the region, but high by OECD standards. Contrary to many LAC countries, informality has been increasing rapidly and now exceeds 45% of total employment (OECD, 2016a). The causes of informality are varied and complex but in part arise from a very weak tax compliance culture and tax administration (Oviedo, 2009). Past work from the IMF showed that rigidities in the labour market and the high tax burden were the most important drivers of informality. The importance of the agricultural sector in the economy and the impact of inflation were also key drivers of the informal sector in Costa Rica (Vuletin, 2008).

Bringing more taxpayers within the formal economy should be a key priority. Due to the size of the informal sector, the tax burden in Costa Rica is borne by a small number of taxpayers. This puts a limit to the amount of tax revenue that can be raised. It also creates distortions between the formal and informal economy and puts a limit to the impact of the tax system in reducing inequality. High informality will typically also result in higher tax rates levied on taxpayers that fall within the tax net, which leads to further efficiency losses.

Ensuring all legal entities and arrangements register with the tax administration, file income tax returns and comply with the general tax system will help combat tax avoidance and evasion. Corporations that do not engage in economic activity in Costa Rica are referred to as "inactive companies". Before 2017, these entities were not always required to comply with the rules of the tax system and did not even have to be registered with the tax administration. Moreover, the ownership of the shares of these companies was only recorded in the books of the entity and the details were frequently not kept up-to-date and the tax administration often did not have information about the beneficial owners of those companies. Inactive companies can be used as vehicles to hide assets, both for tax and non-tax purposes. Costa Rica enacted legislation to require all relevant legal entities and arrangements to maintain registers of beneficial ownership information, and to further require that all registered entities register with the tax administration and pay some level of tax. These legal changes represent a significant improvement by Costa Rica to reduce the risk of tax avoidance and evasion, both domestically and globally. However, Costa Rica must ensure these reforms are successful in the long term by implementing effective supervision programmes that appropriately penalise non-compliance.

Current reforms aimed at reducing tax avoidance and tax evasion are a step in the right direction. Costa Rica's Congress approved two bills which aim at reducing tax avoidance and tax evasion: the "law against tax fraud" and the "legal entities law". The "law against tax fraud" sets out obligations related to the disclosure of information which will enable the tax administration to obtain information on the shareholders and beneficial owners of an entity. The "legal entities law" creates a new tax on legal entities and domestic subsidiaries registered before the National Registry; entities failing to pay the tax for three consecutive years will be liquidated automatically.

The tax and SSC administration should strengthen their co-operation to tackle tax evasion. Revenues from SSCs are collected, administered and subject to audits by the *Caja Costarricense de Seguridad Social* (CCSS), while national taxes are collected, administered and audited by the Ministerio de Hacienda. Strengthening the co-operation – possibly even the integration of the income tax and social security administrations – including through improved information sharing between the tax and SSC administrations, could reduce evasion as firms tend to understate their labour costs to the social security system and overstate them to the tax administration.

Efforts should be made to modernise the tax administration through computerisation, risk-based compliance assessments, and by increasing the number and the training of the staff employed in the tax administration. A system for rapid and transparent dispute resolution should be put in place. There is ample scope to use information and technology (IT) tools more extensively to improve tax collection. Across OECD countries, higher spending on IT is associated with better performance-related indicators, such as e-filing, e-payment and lower tax collection costs (OECD, 2015).

The tax administration needs to strengthen its tax auditing capacities. Calculations by the IADB show that in 2010, among registered taxpayers in Costa Rica, only 0.3% were subject to mass audits per year, and only 0.1% of taxpayers were subject to an in-depth audit while the average in the region was 2.8% and 0.2% respectively (IADB, 2013).

Stronger international tax rules and domestic tax policy reform have to go hand in hand with measures that strengthen the functioning of the tax administration. As the country introduces major tax policy reforms, adopts the OECD/G20 BEPS measures and introduces further changes to its international tax rules, an efficient tax administration is required to put these new tax rules into practice and ensure that the tax burden is shared fairly across all taxpayers. This will also require that effective penalty regimes are put in place to level the playing field between those taxpayers that comply with the tax rules and those who do not.

Tax reform needs to be accompanied by institutional reform

Reforms should limit the degree of revenue earmarking while maintaining the availability and quality of public services. While a certain degree of earmarking might bring advantages, as previously pointed out, the earmarking of tax revenues has become the dominant strategy which jeopardises the well-functioning of government in Costa Rica. Government should review its tax earmarking rules and set in place different governance strategies which ensure that public expenditure receives the appropriate funding. Such a reform should allow government to regain discretionary power in the management of public finances while maintaining social coverage and the quality of public services. While the difficulty associated with such a significant reform is acknowledged, especially given that this requires a Constitutional amendment, this is an important reform that will be needed if Costa Rica is to place itself on a path of fiscal sustainability in the long term.

The PIT and the SSC system need to be integrated. SSC funds can set their own SSC rates in order to balance their budgets and employee SSCs are not deductible from taxable personal income. The lack of integration between the two systems results in very high SSC rates, and therefore high labour income tax burdens, which distorts the labour market significantly. Using SSCs to fund programmes other than social security (e.g. funding of public banks) further increases non-wage related costs, which creates even stronger tax-induced disincentives to enter the formal economy for employees and to create jobs in the formal economy for employers.

The market-based valuation of immovable property across the entire country needs to be included in the reform agenda. Central government is responsible for building and maintaining the fiscal cadastre while the local governments are responsible for the valuation of immovable property. The degree to which immovable property is valued according to the same rules set by central government differs across the country. Central government need to provide support to local governments who lack the capacity to value property. In order to prevent unfair competition, central government needs also to ensure that all local governments apply the same valuation rules.

A fiscal federalism reform would revisit the financial relations between central and local governments. As determined by the Constitution, municipalities in Costa Rica are autonomous (Romero-Perez, 2004). Local governments are entitled to spend the revenues they collect, on the one hand, but they do not receive substantive transfers from the central government, on the other hand. This creates an advantage for larger and richer municipalities and cities over smaller and poorer municipalities, resulting in differences in the quality of local public services across local governments. The lack of a fiscal equalisation mechanism needs to be addressed over time in order to ensure a similar economic development across all regions within the country.

Overview of the planned tax reforms

Costa Rica has been trying to introduce important tax reforms but the legislative process to adopt the income tax and VAT bills has stalled. The last two reforms which were put to Congress have been declared unconstitutional by the Constitutional Court (see Box 1.1).

The current government has put tax reform back on the agenda. The current government has filed 10 tax-related bills before Congress. Contrary to the approach followed by previous administrations, the current administration includes each reform in a separate bill. Some of the tax reforms, yet to be approved, deal with reforming the corporate and personal income tax and the sales tax: the main elements of the PIT, CIT and VAT reforms are presented in Table 1.3.

Box 1.1. **Recent tax reforms in Costa Rica**

Since 1978 all governments have filed tax reform bills before Congress. Even though some minor reforms took place, only three Administrations were able to make significant modifications to the tax system: in 1982 – a sales tax reform; in 1988 – an income tax reform; and between 1995 and1997 – tax procedure reforms. Costa Rica has unsuccessfully tried to reform its income and sales tax several times in the last 12 years.

Under president Abel Pacheco de la Espriella's administration (2002-06), the government filed before Congress a single bill, which aimed at transforming the sales tax into a regular VAT and replacing the schedular income tax with a global income tax. Technically, the bill was very complex and wide-reaching. The Congress created a special commission for its discussion. The reform was approved in a first debate. While approval was pending during a second debate in Congress, the Constitutional Court declared the bill unconstitutional.

Four years later, under president Laura Chinchilla Miranda's administration (2010-14), another major tax reform was put on the agenda. The government filed again one single bill, which included modifications to both the sales tax and the income tax regime; the modifications intended to transform the sales tax into a regular VAT, and replace the scheduler income tax by a dual income tax. The administration reached an agreement with political parties in Congress and the bill was approved during a first debate. However, the Constitutional Court declared that the legislative procedure which was followed was not constitutional and the reform attempt was stopped.

Table 1.3. **Main tax policy reforms before Congress**

Tax bill subject	Most relevant details	Status
Income Tax	• Reduced CIT rates of 10%, 15%, 20% or 25% • Includes foreign-source passive income from non-profitable activities into the CIT base. • Modifies and sets new limits to deductible corporate expenses. • Introduces a limit to the deductibility of net interests equal to 20% of EBITDA. • Carry-forward of corporate losses will be allowed for three years. • Includes procedural amendments such as changing the taxable year to the same as the calendar year. • Increase in the top PIT rate with the inclusion of an additional bracket and rate.	Filed Pending two debates
Sales Tax	• Significant broadening of the tax base to include all services; i.e. turn the sales tax into a genuine VAT. • Significant narrowing of the basic goods exempted from VAT. • A new 4% reduced VAT rate would be introduced on the inputs of some of the goods and services that were previously exempt. • VAT paid on inputs to produce exempt goods and services would no longer be refundable. • Innovative cash transfer system to compensate households in the lowest four income deciles. • The draft VAT bill will request credit and debit card companies to charge VAT on the cross-border purchases of goods, intangibles and services.	Filed Pending two debates
Low carbon vehicles	• Broad tax exemptions for electric vehicles	

The tax policy recommendations that can be drawn from this analysis are as follows:

Recommendations

- Balance the budget through tax reform and spending control.
- Increase tax revenues and gradually rebalance the tax mix when the budget will be balanced.
- Move away from the excessive earmarking of tax revenues.
- Integrate the tax and SSC systems from a tax policy, administrative and auditing perspective.
- Broaden the bases of the major taxes, including the VAT, CIT and PIT.
- Strengthen the role of the tax and transfer system in lowering inequality.
- Strengthen the fight against tax evasion and prevent tax-induced incentives to remain informal.
- Revisit the fiscal federalism relations between central and local governments.
- Modernise the tax administration. Use information and technology (IT) tools more extensively to improve tax collection and better target tax auditing.

References

Adelfang, J. (2016), "Tenemos las peores finanzas pública de Latinoamérica?", [Have we the worst public finances in Latinamerica?], *La Republica,* Oct. 10, 2016, pp. 10-11.

Arenas de Mesa, A. (2016), "Sostenibilidad fiscal y reformas tributarias en América Latina", [Fiscal sustainability and tax reforms in Latinamerica], Santiago: CEPAL, http://repositorio.cepal.org/bitstream/handle/11362/40624/1/S1600733_es.pdf.

Bachas, P. and M. Soto (2016), "Not (ch) your average tax system: corporate taxation under weak enforcement", Working Paper, https://www8.gsb.columbia.edu/faculty-research/sites/faculty-research/files/finance/Applied%20Microeconomics/Fall%202016/Corporate_tax_elasticity_BachasSoto_2016%20(1).pdf.

Global Credit Research (2016), "Moody's Changes Outlook on Costa Rica's Ba1 rating to negative from stable; affirms rating", Moody's, webpage, https://www.moodys.com/research/Moodys-changes-outlook-on-Costa-Ricas-Ba1-rating-to-negative--PR_342961 (accessed 8 December 2016).

González Pandiella, A. (2016), "Making Growth More Inclusive in Costa Rica", *OECD Economics Department Working Papers*, No. 1300, OECD Publishing, Paris, http://dx.doi.org/10.1787/5jlz4043b39w-en.

IADB – División de Gestión Fiscal y Municipal (2015), "Nota de política fiscal", [Fiscal policy notes], Costa Rica.

IADB (2013), "More than revenue. Taxation as a development tool".

IMF (2016), "Costa Rica: selected issues and analytical notes", *IMF Country Report* No. 16/132.

IMF (2015), "Costa Rica. Staff report for the 2014 Article IV consultation", *IMF Country Report* No. 15/29.

IMF (2013), "Costa Rica Selected Issues", *IMF Country Report* No. 13/80.

Melguizo A., S. Nieto-Parra, J.R. Perea and J. Perez (forthcoming), "No sympathy for the devil: policy priorities to overcome the middle-income trap in Latin America", *OECD Development Centre Working Papers*, OECD Publishing, Paris.

Ministerio de Hacienda (2017), *Gobierno Central Detalle*, [Details of the central government], www.hacienda.go.cr/contenido/12520-gobierno-central-detalle (accessed 7 February 2017).

Ministerio de Hacienda (2016), *El Presupuesto Nacional en Costa Rica*, [National budget in Costa Rica], San José de Costa Rica.

Ministerio de Hacienda (2014), *El Gasto Tributario, Metodología Y Estimación*, [Tax expenditure, methodology and estimations], San José de Costa Rica.

OECD (2016a), *OECD Economic Surveys: Costa Rica 2016: Economic Assessment*, OECD Publishing, Paris, http://dx.doi.org/10.1787/eco_surveys-cri-2016-en.

OECD (2016b), *Revenue Statistics 2016*, OECD Publishing, Paris, http://dx.doi.org/10.1787/rev_stats-2016-en-fr.

OECD (2015), *Tax Administration 2015: Comparative Information on OECD and Other Advanced and Emerging Economies*, OECD Publishing, Paris, http://dx.doi.org/10.1787/tax_admin-2015-en.

OECD/ECLAC/CIAT/IDB (2017), *Revenue Statistics in Latin America and the Caribbean 2017*, OECD Publishing, Paris, http://dx.doi.org/10.1787/rev_lat_car-2017-en-fr.

OECD/ECLAC/CAF (2016), *Latin American Economic Outlook 2017: Youth, Skills and Entrepreneurship*, OECD Publishing, Paris, http://dx.doi.org/10.1787/leo-2017-en.

Oviedo, A.-M. (2009), *Economic Informality: Causes, Costs, and Policies. A Literature Survey of International Experience*, World Bank, http://siteresources.worldbank.org/TURKEYEXTN/Resources/361711-1277211666558/bpg_CausesCostsAndPolicies.pdf.

Perry, G., E. Maloney, F. William et al. (2007), *Informality: Exit and Exclusion*, Latin American and Caribean Studies, The World Bank, Washington, DC, https://openknowledge.worldbank.org/handle/10986/6730, License: CC BY 3.0 IGO.

Romero-Perez, J. (2004), *La Autonomía Constitucional de las Municipalidades*, [Constitutional autonomy of municipalities], Ponencia al Congreso Internacional de Estudios Municipales, Escuela de Administración Pública, San José de Costa Rica, 18-20 February 2004.

The World Bank Group (2015), "Country partnership framework for the Republic of Costa Rica for the period FY16-FY20", Report No. 94686-CR, The World Bank Group, Washington D.C., https://openknowledge.worldbank.org/handle/10986/23124.

UNCTAD (2016), *Foreign Direct Investment: Inward and Outward Flows and Stock, Annual, 1970-2015*, Stat (database), http://unctadstat.unctad.org/wds/TableViewer/tableView.aspx (accessed 22 November 2016) UNCTAD.

Vuletin, G. (2008), "Measuring the Informal Economy in Latin America and the Caribbean", *IMF Working Paper* 08/102, Western Hemisphere Department, April 2008.

Chapter 2

Reforming the corporate tax system in Costa Rica

This chapter discusses the corporate income tax (CIT) in Costa Rica, focusing on CIT rates and the main CIT base provisions including tax depreciation allowances. Corporate effective tax rate (ETR) calculations show the combined impact of CIT provisions on the effective tax burden on investment in Costa Rica. The chapter discusses the debt-equity bias, the taxation of foreign-source passive income and the country's narrow tax treaty network. The chapter analyses whether the tax system creates a tax-induced incentive for foreign direct investment (FDI) in Costa Rica and analyses the impact on the ETRs of the CIT incentives for companies located in the Free Trade Zones (FTZ); the analysis distinguishes between parent companies which are tax resident in a country with a worldwide or a territorial tax system.

Domestic-source profits are taxed at high standard tax rates but raise relatively little revenue

Costa Rica implements a pure territorial CIT system. Resident and non-resident companies are taxed under the CIT on the income which has its source within the country. Any foreign-source income, earned by either resident or non-resident companies, is not taxed under the CIT in Costa Rica; this exemption applies to active and passive foreign-source income. This turns the Costa Rican CIT system into a pure territorial tax system.

Costa Rica levies a high standard statutory CIT tax. The top statutory CIT rate is 30%, which is higher than the standard CIT rate on average in the Latin-America and the Caribbean (LAC) region (26%) and in the OECD (24.7%) in 2016. On average, smaller countries in the OECD tend to implement lower standard CIT rates; Costa Rica implements lower CIT rates only for small and medium size enterprises (SMEs).

Lower CIT rates apply to SMEs. Costa Rica currently implements two reduced CIT rates. The CIT rate is levied on taxable income at a rate of 10% for firms with annual gross income up to CRC 52.32 million; the rate is 20% for firms with annual gross income between CRC 52.32 million and CRC 105.241 million above which the standard 30% rate applies. About half of the OECD countries levy a reduced CIT rate for SMEs, reducing country's CIT rates on average by about 4 percentage points (OECD, 2015a). Reduced CIT rates for SMEs can also be found in some countries in the LAC region (see Table 2.1).

The Costa Rican reduced CIT rate schedule for SMEs has uncommon design features. The reduced CIT rate schedule has multiple reduced rates. The relevant rate is established according to companies' gross income but the tax liability is determined by applying the rate to taxable income. Empirical analysis (Bachas and Soto, 2016) using Costa Rican tax return data has found that the design of the Costa Rican CIT rate schedule has resulted in clear bunching of firms below each of the turnover thresholds; by underreporting revenues, corporations can benefit from a reduced CIT rate levied on their taxable income. There is clear evidence that firms in Costa Rica not only deflate revenues in order to benefit from a reduced CIT rate but also inflate costs to reduce their taxable income.

In fact, using size-based thresholds is not necessarily an effective tool to support investment and may restrain growth. The creation of tax preferences can introduce additional complexity and distortions into the tax system. For example, thresholds limiting tax preferences to entities under a certain size can create barriers to the growth of SMEs. Size-based tax preferences give businesses incentives to remain below the threshold so as to continue benefiting from such targeted regimes, both in terms of reduced compliance costs as well as tax payable (OECD, 2015a). Growing SMEs or larger companies may be incentivised to split up into different companies to benefit from the preferential tax treatment or to engage in deflating revenues and inflating costs. Such regimes may also provide windfall gains to businesses that, for various reasons, may not be likely to invest and grow. Finally, when reduced rates are based on turnover, they tend to penalise low profit-margin business, which end up being taxed at a higher rate than businesses with a lower turnover but higher profits.

Costa Rica plans to significantly reform its reduced CIT rate schedule for SMEs as part of its tax reform proposal. A double test would apply. First, only firms with turnover below CRC 106 million (about EUR 179 000) would benefit from the reduced CIT rate schedule for SMEs. Second, the reduced CIT rate would no longer vary with turnover but with taxable income. The reduced CIT rate would be 10%, 15%, 20% or 25%; the 25% rate would be levied on taxable income exceeding CRC 10 million (i.e. EUR 16 900).

Table 2.1. **Statutory CIT rate, withholding tax rates on dividends and interest paid to non-residents and number of tax treaties for a selection of LAC countries**

	Statutory CIT rate	Withholding tax rate on dividends	Withholding tax rate on interest	Number of treaties
Costa Rica	10/20/30 a	15	15	2
Belize	25	15	15	13
El Salvador	25/30 b	5	20	1
Guatemala	25	5	10	0
Honduras	25/30 c	10	10	0
Nicaragua	30	7.5 g	7.5 g	0
Panama	25	10 h	12.5 h	16
Dominican Rep.	27	10	10	2
Ecuador	22	0 i	22	19
Uruguay	25	7	12	18
Argentina	35	10	35	19
Brazil	24/34 d	0 j	15	33
Chile	24 e	35 e	4/35 l	32
Colombia	34/40 f	0 k	15 m	13
Mexico	30	10	35	56
Peru	28	6.8	30	11

Notes: a. CIT rates vary by gross income; starting from CRC 105 241,000 the rate is 30%.

b. The general CIT rate is 30%; it is reduced to 25% only when taxable income does not exceed USD 150 000.

c. The general CIT rate is 25%; companies with taxable income exceeding HNL 1 million (about EUR 41 000) are subject to a 5% surtax.

d. The general CIT rate is 15%; in addition, there is a social contribution tax of 9% and a 10% surtax for companies with taxable income above BRL 240 000.

e. The general CIT rate is 24%; dividends distributed to non-residents receive a tax credit for corporate income taxes paid and are subject to a 35% withholding tax.

f. The general CIT rate is 34% (for year 2017). In addition, companies with taxable income above COP 800 million face an additional surtax of 6% (for year 2017).

g. Withholding tax rates on dividends and interest are 15% on 50% of the gross amount.

h. Withholding tax rates on interest are 25% on 50% of the gross amount. Withholding tax on dividends is 10% if the income distributed is Panamanian-source, 5% if it is foreign-source income, and 20% in case of bearer shares.

i. Withholding tax on dividends is zero if paid out of taxed profits and 22% otherwise.

j. Withholding tax on dividends is zero if paid out of taxed profits and 15% otherwise.

k. Withholding tax on dividends is zero if paid out of taxed profits and 35% otherwise.

l. A reduced rate of 4% withholding tax on interest is available for loans granted by foreign banks, insurance companies or financial institutions.

m. Withholding tax rates on interest are taxed at 15%; a reduced rate of 5% is levied on interest payments for loans exceeding a 8-year term for the funding of public infrastructure works under public private partnerships.

Source: Own Research, IBFD.

Costa Rica has very few tax treaties which lower the withholding tax rates on dividends and interest payments to non-residents. In addition to the CIT rate, countries levy withholding tax rates on dividends and interest payments to non-residents; see Table 2.1 for the standard tax rates that apply in a selection of LAC countries. Tax treaties typically apply lower withholding tax rates on dividends and interest payments to non-residents but, as can be seen from Table 2.1, countries differ significantly in the number of tax treaties they have in place. Three countries – Ecuador, Brazil and Colombia – impose withholding tax rates only on dividends paid out of profits which have not been subject to CIT. Among the remaining countries, standard withholding tax rates on dividends vary between 5% and 35%. Withholding tax rates on interest payments are typically higher than those on dividends, ranging between 10% and 35%. Withholding tax rates in Costa Rica are 5% if made by a company listed in Costa Rica and 15% for companies which are not listed in Costa Rica (i.e. the 15% rate applies to dividend payments by a non-listed host company to its parent company located in another jurisdiction). The latter rate is higher than for many neighbouring countries, in particular because the country has only two tax treaties in place (with Spain and Germany).

Despite the high standard CIT rate, CIT revenues in Costa Rica are low. The CIT base in Costa Rica is narrow as a result of high tax evasion, a large informal sector and a wide-range of tax incentives. Recent evidence (Bachas and Soto, 2016) shows that the reduced CIT rates in Costa Rica result in significant tax evasion. In addition, Costa Rica provides a wide-range of tax incentives in particular for companies in Free Trade Zones (FTZ) and for not-for-profit organisations. As a result of the narrow CIT base and the significant tax evasion, CIT revenues in Costa Rica amounted to only 2.2% of GDP in 2014, which is significantly lower than CIT revenues on average in the LAC region and the OECD (see Figure 2.1).

Figure 2.1. **Corporate income tax revenues as a % of GDP, 2014**

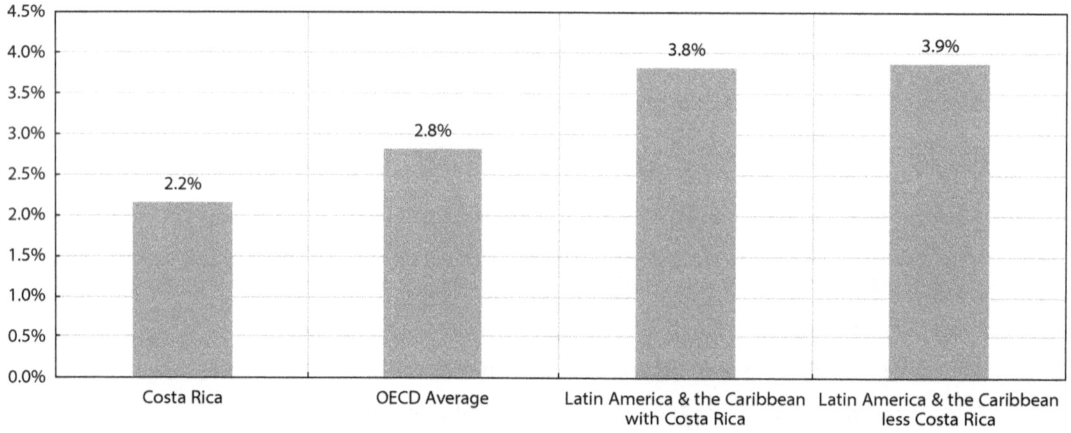

StatLink http://dx.doi.org/10.1787/888933544664

Source: OECD Revenue Statistics database.

The depreciation of assets for tax purposes can be simplified

Costa Rica applies standard tax depreciation methods but the tax depreciation rates vary widely across similar assets. The historical costs of assets can be depreciated either following the straight-line or the sum-of-the-year's-digits method. Other tax depreciation methods can be applied but need to be approved on a case-by-case basis by the tax administration; this follows common OECD practice. However, the tax code foresees over 500 categories of assets. For instance, the tax code distinguishes between 12 categories of machinery and equipment. Machinery and equipment in the rice-growing sector needs to be depreciated at a rate of 7% while the same assets in the rest of the agricultural sector can be depreciated at a rate of 10%; similar types of assets in the building sector face a 15% tax depreciation rate. The differentiation across industries of similar assets is rarely found in OECD countries. Such sophisticated differentiation makes the tax depreciation system very complex and increases tax compliance and administration costs.

In order to simplify compliance and administration costs related to tax depreciation, Costa Rica could divide assets into broad asset classes. Instead of setting tax depreciation rates on an asset-by-asset basis, Costa Rica could group similar types of assets (such as machinery and equipment, buildings, assets used for transport, intangible assets, etc.) within broad asset classes. The asset classes could be defined such that the assets included in the class would face a relatively similar economic depreciation rate. Such an approach would allow similar types of assets to be depreciated for tax purposes in the same way across different industries. Tax depreciation rates could be set as close as possible to the economic depreciation of the asset (OECD, 2007). Such a reform would contribute to the broadening of the tax base and reduce distortions in capital allocation across assets and industries.

Corporations face an incentive to finance investment with debt rather than equity

Resident corporations face a tax-induced incentive to finance investment with debt. As in most countries, interest payments are deductible from the CIT base but the return on equity is not, which creates a tax-induced incentive to finance investment with debt rather than equity. Dividends paid by a Costa Rican corporation to a domestic corporation are exempt from CIT (at the recipient level), irrespective of whether CIT has effectively been paid. Interest paid to resident companies is taxed as ordinary business income in the hands of the recipient and subject to the corporation's CIT rate. However, an 8% final withholding tax applies over interest on securities registered with a stock exchange in Costa Rica or issued by a registered financial institution in the country.

The debt bias persists when taxes on capital income at the individual level are taken into account. Dividends paid by a publicly traded company in Costa Rica to (resident or non-resident) individuals are subject to a 5% final withholding tax; i.e. no additional tax is levied on distributed dividends at the personal level for domestic shareholders or creditors. Dividends paid by a non-publicly traded corporation to (resident or non-resident) individuals are subject to a 15% final withholding tax. The tax policy rationale for this differential tax treatment is not very clear; in fact, it creates a tax-induced distortion in favour of larger, more international businesses which are more likely listed on the stock market against smaller non-listed domestic businesses. Given a standard CIT rate of 30%, the combined statutory tax burden on dividends equals 33.5% for listed companies and 40.5% for non-listed companies. Interests paid to (resident or non-resident) individuals are subject to a 15% final withholding tax but an 8% withholding tax applies when interests are paid over securities listed on the national bond market. Capital gains are taxed only if they are part of the business's habitual profitable activity, but are not taxed at the individual shareholder level. Despite the absence of a capital gains tax at the individual level, effective tax rate calculations show that debt remains the most preferred source of finance for domestic corporations (see Box 2.1).

The tax code stimulates also intra-group debt financing in case of a non-resident parent company. Dividend distributions to non-resident corporations are taxed in a similar way as the dividends paid to individuals; i.e. a 5% or 15% withholding tax applies for listed and non-listed corporations, respectively. Costa Rican source interest, commission fees and other financial expenses paid to non-residents corporations are subject to a 15% final withholding tax. The slightly higher withholding tax on interest does not offset the CIT advantage of debt compared to equity-financing. Foreign parent companies may therefore prefer financing their subsidiary in Costa Rica with debt rather than equity.

The corporate debt bias distorts corporate financing and investment decisions. The differential tax treatment of debt and equity provides corporations with a tax-induced incentive to finance investment with debt rather than equity. This may make companies more prone to insolvency and discriminates against small companies and start-ups, which may have reduced access to debt financing or would have to borrow at higher rates (OECD, 2007). It may also imply that highly innovative businesses whose main asset is knowledge capital may face a higher cost of financing than mature companies. Also corporate firms that own firm-specific assets against which it is difficult to borrow suffer a tax-induced competitive disadvantage (Cnossen, 1996).

Costa Rica faces wide ranging ETRs on domestic investment

Corporate ETR calculations show the combined impact of tax provisions on the effective tax burdens on investment in Costa Rica. Box 2.1 presents effective tax rates on domestic investment in Costa Rica; the results capture the impact of the standard and reduced statutory CIT rates, the tax depreciation allowances for different types of assets (i.e. investment in non-residential buildings, machinery and equipment and intangible assets) and the taxes on capital income at the individual level. The analysis presents results for both listed and non-listed companies to capture the effect of different withholding tax rates on dividends.

Corporate ETR calculations for domestic investment confirm the tax financing ranking order: corporations face a tax-induced incentive to finance investment with debt over equity; retained earnings are preferred to newly issued equity as a source of finance (see Box 2.1). Indeed, a clear pattern emerges from the comparison of ETRs across financing sources. First, investments financed by new equity are generally subject to higher ETRs. This result is due to the withholding taxes levied on distributions from publicly traded or non-publicly traded companies. Second, ETRs for investments financed through retained earnings are considerably lower due to the fact that taxation of dividends at the personal level reduces the opportunity cost for this type of financing and because Costa Rica does not levy a capital gains tax at the individual shareholder level. However, interest deductibility implies that debt-financed investments are the most tax-favoured type of investment, especially for firms in the upper tax brackets. Taken together, the tax system thus discourages investments financed by new equity compared to debt finance. For smaller, possibly credit-constrained firms the difference is less significant; however, it becomes substantial for firms in the upper two tax brackets.

Box 2.1. Costa Rica: Effective tax rates on domestic investment

Economic model and assumptions

Forward-looking ETRs are an important tax policy measure capturing information on tax rates and bases as well as other relevant provisions within a comparable framework. A well-established methodology exists to calculate ETRs on the basis of prospective, or hypothetical, investment projects. The modelling approach used to calculate effective tax rates for investments in Costa Rica builds on the standard theoretical framework developed by Devereux and Griffith (1999, 2003) and is described in detail in Hanappi (forthcoming). Building on the economic literature, the OECD model for the calculation of corporate ETRs combines information on

Box 2.1. **Costa Rica: Effective tax rates on domestic investment** *(continued)*

tax rules (e.g. tax depreciation and incentives) with a set of asset-specific information and other economic assumptions (e.g. rates of return and economic depreciation). Two types of effective tax rates are calculated:

- Effective marginal tax rates (EMTRs) measure the extent to which taxation increases the pre-tax rate of return required by investors to break even. This indicator is used to analyse investment decisions at the intensive margin, that is, to assess how taxes affect the incentive to expand investment given a fixed location.
- Effective average tax rates (EATRs) measure the effect of taxation on investment projects earning economic profits; it is based on a comparison of the net present value of pre-tax and post-tax cash flows. This indicator is used to analyse investment decisions at the extensive margin, that is, location decisions; e.g. when a multinational decides to locate a plant in one of many jurisdictions.

Three sources of finance are considered: retained earnings, new equity and debt. The ETR calculations presented in this analysis focus on domestic investment in Costa Rica by listed and non-listed corporations. Apart from the ETRs, results are also shown for the **cost of capital**, which is defined as the real pre-tax rate of return to generate a zero post-tax economic rent; as such it is linked to the EMTR.

The prospective investment project is described by the pre-tax rate of return and economic depreciation:

- The **pre-tax rate of return** determines income, net of variable costs and depreciation, earned from a given capital stock. The EATRs, which measure tax effects on projects earning economic rents, will be increasing in the pre-tax rate of return. Because the EMTRs measure the tax burden on marginal investments which, by definition, just breaks even, the pre-tax rate of return does not have an impact on the EMTRs. In the context of Costa Rica, an upper middle income country with an average growth rate just below 4% in the last 5 years, the pre-tax rate of return is assumed to be 20%.
- **Economic depreciation** determines the lifetime and, hence, the profitability of the investment project in terms of its Net Present Value (NPV). The calculations presented in this section are based on three stylised assets: (1) non-residential buildings depreciating under the declining balance method at a rate of 3%; (2) machinery and equipment depreciating at 8%; and (3) an intangible asset depreciating at 25%.

Three **tax depreciation schedules** are considered: (1) straight line depreciation at 2% for non-residential buildings; (2) straight line depreciation at 10% for machinery and equipment; and (3) straight line depreciation at 20% for intangible assets. These parameters are based on a recent OECD questionnaire on capital investment modelling in which Costa Rica has taken part in March 2016, capturing tax rules as of July 2015. Comparing tax depreciation rules with the economic depreciation of the corresponding assets shows that tax depreciation is slightly decelerated for non-residential structures, moderately accelerated for machinery and equipment, and decelerated for intangible assets.

The two main economic parameters of relevance are the **real interest rate** and **inflation**. Both parameters interact with each other as well as with tax parameters and financial flows. For the calculations presented in this section both parameters, real interest and inflation, are assumed to be equal to their 5-year average for Costa Rica (2011-15). Correspondingly, the **real interest rate** has been set to 12% and **inflation** to 3.5%.

Empirical results

The results are shown in Tables 2.2 and 2.3. Each table includes EATRs, EMTRs and the cost of capital (CoC) for all nine combinations of tax brackets and asset types given the source of finance. Several results emerge from the analysis:

- Comparing results between different assets shows that both ETRs are higher for assets subject to decelerated depreciation, i.e. non-residential structures and intangibles. Differences in the EATR compared to the second asset, machinery and equipment, can be up to 4 percentage points for firms in the highest tax bracket; difference in the EMTR can be up to 5 percentage points for the retained earnings case and 7 percentage points for debt-financed investments.

Box 2.1. **Costa Rica: Effective tax rates on domestic investment** *(continued)*

- Comparing the EATRs for a specific asset across tax brackets shows that increases in the statutory CIT rate of 10 percentage points lead to corresponding increases in EATRs of around 8-10 percentage points for equity-financed investments (retained earnings or new equity). However, for debt-financed investments the increase in the EATRs is much lower, around 2-3 percentage points, since interest deductibility implies that higher statutory rates also increase the value of the interest that can be deducted from the corporate tax base.
- Withholding tax rates reduce the opportunity cost of retained earnings in terms of foregone dividends. As a result, EATRs on investments financed by retained earnings are lower than on investments which are financed by new equity. While this difference is more pronounced (around 10 percentage points) in case of non-publicly traded companies, which are subject to a 15% withholding tax rate on dividends, it is also visible for publicly traded companies, which are subject to 5% withholding tax.
- For equity-financed investments the EMTRs are generally quite close to the EATRs; this is due to two factors. On the one hand, tax depreciation schedules largely follow real economic depreciation; only investments in machinery and equipment are subject to acceleration while the other two assets follow slightly decelerated schedules. On the other hand, our assumptions about interest rates and inflation imply that the nominal interest rate and thus the shareholder's discount rate is relatively high; economic rents earned in future periods are thus less valuable in present terms, reducing the difference between the respective average and marginal rates. EMTRs on debt-financed investments are very low, especially for investments in machinery and equipment which are subject to a slightly accelerated tax depreciation schedule.

Table 2.2. **ETRs on domestic investment (listed companies)**

	Retained earnings								
	CIT 10%			CIT 20%			CIT 30%		
	Buildings	Machinery	Intangibles	Buildings	Machinery	Intangibles	Buildings	Machinery	Intangibles
EATR	5.8	4.5	5.7	16.0	13.4	15.7	26.1	22.3	25.7
EMTR	10.9	8.7	10.7	21.6	17.6	21.2	32.1	26.8	31.6
CoC	12.1	11.8	12.1	13.7	13.1	13.7	15.9	14.7	15.7

	New equity								
	CIT 10%			CIT 20%			CIT 30%		
	Buildings	Machinery	Intangibles	Buildings	Machinery	Intangibles	Buildings	Machinery	Intangibles
EATR	9.4	8.1	9.2	19.5	16.9	19.1	29.7	25.7	29.0
EMTR	16.0	13.9	15.7	25.2	21.5	24.7	34.6	29.7	34.0
CoC	12.8	12.5	12.8	14.4	13.7	14.3	16.5	15.3	16.3

	Debt								
	CIT 10%			CIT 20%			CIT 30%		
	Buildings	Machinery	Intangibles	Buildings	Machinery	Intangibles	Buildings	Machinery	Intangibles
EATR	4.3	3.1	4.2	7.1	4.7	7.2	9.9	6.5	10.4
EMTR	8.7	6.3	8.4	11.0	6.0	10.9	17.7	10.4	17.9
CoC	11.8	11.5	11.8	12.1	11.5	12.1	13.1	12.0	13.1

Note: 5% withholding tax rate applies to dividends; 8% withholding tax rate applies to interest.

Box 2.1. **Costa Rica: Effective tax rates on domestic investment** *(continued)*

Table 2.3. **ETRs on domestic investment (non-listed companies)**

	Retained earnings								
	CIT 10%			CIT 20%			CIT 30%		
	Buildings	Machinery	Intangibles	Buildings	Machinery	Intangibles	Buildings	Machinery	Intangibles
EATR	4.4	3.3	4.3	13.6	11.4	13.4	22.8	19.5	22.5
EMTR	11.0	8.7	10.8	21.8	17.6	21.5	32.4	26.8	31.9
CoC	10.9	10.6	10.9	12.4	11.8	12.3	14.3	13.2	14.2

	New equity								
	CIT 10%			CIT 20%			CIT 30%		
	Buildings	Machinery	Intangibles	Buildings	Machinery	Intangibles	Buildings	Machinery	Intangibles
EATR	14.4	13.3	14.2	23.6	21.2	23.0	32.7	29.2	31.9
EMTR	26.2	24.5	25.9	32.9	29.7	32.3	40.2	35.8	39.5
CoC	13.1	12.8	13.1	14.5	13.8	14.3	16.2	15.1	16.0

	Debt								
	CIT 10%			CIT 20%			CIT 30%		
	Buildings	Machinery	Intangibles	Buildings	Machinery	Intangibles	Buildings	Machinery	Intangibles
EATR	7.8	6.6	7.6	10.3	8.1	10.2	12.8	9.8	13.1
EMTR	16.8	14.7	16.5	17.2	12.6	17.0	22.1	15.0	22.1
CoC	11.6	11.4	11.6	11.7	11.1	11.7	12.4	11.4	12.4

Note: 15% withholding tax rate applies to dividends; 15% withholding tax rate applies to interest.

A broad capital income tax reform could contribute to addressing the debt-equity bias

Costa Rica faces different tax policy options to address the debt-equity bias and to integrate the corporate and personal level taxes on distributed profits. *Dividend deduction systems* provide for a partial or full deduction of dividends from taxable corporate profits. *Split-rate CIT systems* levy a lower CIT rate on distributed profits than on retained profits. *Dividend imputation systems* provide tax relief at the individual level for the CIT paid on distributed dividends. Under a dividend imputation system, dividends are grossed up with (part of) the CIT already paid, after which the grossed-up dividends are taxed at the individual shareholder level. The dividend tax is then reduced with (part of) the CIT with which the net dividends were grossed up in the first place. Finally, dividends can also be taxed at lower effective rates than interest payments under a *schedular tax treatment*, either by including only part of the dividends in taxable personal income or by taxing dividends at lower tax rates than interest payments.

Belgium and Italy have introduced an Allowance for Corporate Equity (ACE) to address the debt-equity bias. An ACE tax system corrects for the differential tax treatment of debt and equity by providing a deductible allowance for corporate equity in computing the corporation's taxable profits. Similarly to the deductibility of interest payments from the CIT base, the ACE equals the value of the corporation's equity times an appropriate interest rate. The allowance therefore approximates the corporation's "normal" profits; the CIT rate is then confined to economic rents because corporate equity in excess of the ACE remains subject to corporate tax. In order to prevent windfall gains for existing capital owners, and to reduce its cost in the short and medium-run, the ACE could be provided only to new investment (as is the case in Italy) and not to the existing capital stock (as is the case in Belgium) (OECD, 2007).

Costa Rica should not address the debt-equity bias through the introduction of an ACE in the short run. The ACE is costly in terms of tax revenue foregone. Moreover, if not well-designed, the ACE leads to strategic tax planning opportunities which put CIT revenues further under pressure. The introduction of the ACE therefore requires anti-avoidance rules and strict tax enforcement. Because of the corresponding tax administrative challenges and the fact that Costa Rica needs to raise more revenues to balance its budget, the country should not aim at introducing an ACE in the short run.

Over time, Costa Rica could start taxing capital income at the individual level instead of levying final withholding taxes on capital income at the corporate level as currently is the case. An interesting tax policy option for Costa Rica would be the introduction of a Dual Income Tax (DIT) (Brys, et.al, 2016). Under a DIT, capital and labour income are taxed under a separate tax rate schedule. Taxing capital income at the individual level would allow taxing capital income at progressive tax rates and/ or foresee a basic allowance which exempts a minimum amount of capital income from tax – most countries which implement a DIT tax capital income at proportional rates – thereby strengthening the fairness of the tax system. It would allow shifting the capital income tax burden partly from the corporate level towards the individual level, which would allow lowering the standard CIT rate and aligning the rate in Costa Rica with the CIT rates in other LAC and OECD countries. Such a reform would also allow aligning the top tax burden on capital and labour income in order to prevent large tax-induced incentives for employers to incorporate. However, such a reform would come at significant administrative costs and may therefore not be an immediate tax reform priority for the country.

In light of the broader fiscal challenges which Costa Rica is facing, the debt-equity bias could best be addressed, at least in the short run, by taxing interest payments at higher withholding rates. As Costa Rica has to increase the amount of tax revenues it raises in order to balance its budget, reforms that reduce the debt-equity bias should not come at a tax revenue cost. In Costa Rica, interest payments are taxed at a low withholding tax rate of 8% or at a rate of 15% for bonds not listed on the bond market, while dividends of listed and unlisted companies are taxed at 5% and 15%, respectively. In order to reduce the debt-equity bias, Costa Rica could therefore consider increasing the withholding tax on interest payments to, at least, 15% but preferably to a slightly higher tax rate.

Costa Rica does not currently apply any limit to the amount of interest expense that is deductible from the CIT base. In contrast to most LAC and OECD countries, businesses can deduct all interest expense from taxable corporate profits. This makes the CIT in Costa Rica vulnerable to Base Erosion and Profit Shifting (BEPS). Because of the high standard CIT rate, international businesses that are highly leveraged can strip profits easily out of the country and realise a significant tax reduction.

The BEPS Project under its Action 4 has established a common approach to the design of rules to prevent excessive interest deductibility. Even though the common approach does not aim at correcting for the debt-equity bias but at reducing profit shifting, it does set a limit to the deductibility of interest and, therefore, indirectly reduces the corporate debt bias. The OECD/G20 BEPS project has recommended implementing interest limitation rules that are profit-based (i.e. interest barriers) rather than balanced sheet based. The common approach is based on a fixed ratio rule which limits an entity's net deductions for interest and payments economically equivalent to interest to a percentage of its earnings before interest, taxes, depreciation and amortisation (EBITDA). Interest between 10% and 30% of EBITDA would remain deductible while the excess interest could be carried forward indefinitely (OECD, 2015f). The common approach also includes a group ratio rule alongside the fixed ratio rule, which would allow an entity with net interest expense above a country's fixed ratio rule to deduct interest up to the level of the net interest/ EBITDA ratio of its worldwide group.

Following international best practices, Costa Rica plans to introduce a profit-based interest limitation rule. Costa Rica's current CIT reform proposal plans to introduce a limit to the deductibility of net interests equal to 20% of EBITDA. Any excess interest expense can be carried forward indefinitely. The tax reform proposal does not foresee an additional group ratio rule. The draft tax bill excludes interest paid on loans used to finance public projects as long as the project developer is tax resident in Costa Rica. The limit does not apply to the banking sector either.

Costa Rica should consider including an additional group ratio rule. This would allow an entity with net interest expense above a country's fixed ratio to deduct interest up to the level of the net interest/EBITDA ratio of its worldwide group. A fixed ratio rule provides a country with a level of protection against BEPS, but it is a blunt tool which does not take into account the fact that groups operating in different sectors may require different amounts of leverage, and even within a sector some groups are more highly leveraged for non-tax reasons. If a benchmark fixed ratio is set at a level appropriate to tackle BEPS, it could lead to double taxation for groups which as a whole are leveraged above this level. Therefore, countries are encouraged to combine a robust and effective fixed ratio rule with a group ratio rule which allows an entity to deduct more interest expense in certain circumstances. A group ratio rule may be introduced as a separate provision from the fixed ratio rule, or as an integral part of an overall rule including both fixed ratio and group ratio tests (OECD, 2015f).

Costa Rica could consider taxing capital gains more broadly under the CIT

Costa Rica taxes capital gains under the CIT if they are earned from the business's habitual business activity or from the sale of depreciable assets. The term "habitual" has been defined by the Constitutional Court rather narrowly as the business's predominant activity that is carried out in a public and frequent manner and to which it dedicates most of its time. Any capital gain which does not meet this specification is not taxed under the CIT; this includes the capital gains earned on the transfer of land.

Broadening the capital gains tax base within the CIT would simplify the CIT and reduce tax avoidance opportunities. Taxing capital gains more broadly will also reduce the administration's tax enforcement efforts. The recent tax reform proposals would abolish the differentiation between habitual and non-habitual business activities, which is a welcome reform. However, the reform plans to tax capital gains at a reduced CIT rate of 12%, which continues to provide businesses a tax-induced incentive to transform regular income into capital gains. Instead of taxing capital gains at a reduced CIT rate, Costa Rica should consider taxing them at the corporation's standard CIT rate instead.

Costa Rica could start taxing foreign-source passive income

There are considerable cross-country differences in the taxation of cross-border income. World-wide tax systems, on the one hand, tax corporations on their worldwide income. Territorial tax systems, on the other hand, tax only the income which has its source in the country. In practice, most countries apply a combination of both systems. In 2012, 28 of the 34 OECD member countries had adopted a territorial tax system exempting most active earnings repatriated from subsidiaries resident in (some or all) host countries. OECD member countries commonly require 10% ownership of a foreign affiliate's shares to qualify for the territorial exemption. Most OECD member countries with territorial tax systems exempt active income earned by foreign affiliates as well as gains on the sale of foreign affiliate shares. Some OECD member countries with territorial tax systems limit the exemption to affiliates resident in countries with which they have a tax treaty.

Costa Rica implements a pure territorial CIT system which taxes only the income which has its source within Costa Rica. Any active or passive income which has its source outside Costa Rica is not taxed under the Costa Rican CIT. This means that Costa Rica implements a full participation exemption regime under which dividends received from abroad remain untaxed in Costa Rica, irrespective of the size of the participation.

Costa Rica needs to set clear rules of what constitutes domestic and foreign-source income. Clear definitions of territoriality prevent tax uncertainty and tax disputes on whether income has its source in Costa Rica or abroad. There have been a number of cases where the tax administration has re-characterised foreign source income as Costa Rican source income.[1] Any future changes to Costa Rica's territorial tax system, such as a move towards the taxation of foreign-source passive income, should be put in place through clear tax legislation leaving as little room as possible for misinterpretation by businesses and the tax administration.

Costa Rica should avoid moving from a territorial towards a full worldwide CIT system which taxes all types of foreign-source, i.e. **both passive and active business income.** The current territorial tax system and the high statutory CIT rate induces Costa Rican businesses to serve foreign markets that levy a low statutory CIT rate from within those markets rather than exporting those goods and services from Costa Rica. However, taxing foreign source active income at a rate as high as 30% would put Costa Rican businesses which compete on foreign markets at a competitive disadvantage. Moreover, Costa Rica is a small open economy and a net importer of capital. It has a relatively low share of tax resident businesses earning income abroad. Under these circumstances, the move towards a full worldwide CIT system would not bring many economic advantages. A move towards a full worldwide tax system would also come at high administrative costs without raising significant tax revenues.

Costa Rica could consider taxing foreign-source passive investment income under the CIT. Because foreign source passive investment income (interest, dividends or royalties) is not taxed in Costa Rica, tax-resident businesses may face tax-induced incentives to invest their profits in financial assets abroad instead of reinvesting them in Costa Rica and finance domestic investment with debt rather than equity, in particular because the CIT rate is relatively high in Costa Rica. By bringing foreign-source passive income within the reach of the CIT, Costa Rica would reduce opportunities for tax avoidance/ evasion as there would no longer be an incentive to re-characterise domestic passive income as foreign-sourced income.

Taxing foreign-source passive investment income at a low rate in Costa Rica will yield low tax revenues. Passive income will be taxed in the host country where the income has its source under that country's CIT and/ or the host country's withholding tax rates when the payments are made to the Costa Rican tax resident corporation. Tax treaties typically reduce the withholding tax rates which apply. However, Costa Rica has only two tax treaties that have entered into force (with Spain and Germany). This implies that for all other countries, standard (i.e. higher) withholding tax rates will be levied. Moreover, in order to prevent double taxation, Costa Rica will have to provide for double tax relief (i.e. to compensate for the fact that the payments already have been taxed at source). As a result, Costa Rica will very likely not raise much revenue from the taxation of foreign-source passive income, in particular if it were to provide double tax relief not only for foreign withholding taxes paid but also for the CIT, although the latter would be rather uncommon with respect to foreign-source passive income.

But taxing foreign-source passive income at a too high rate may be very distortive, in particular because a high tax rate may lower the competitiveness of domestic Costa Rican corporations who invest abroad and it may induce businesses to defer the repatriation of funds back to Costa Rica. It therefore is also important that the new tax rules do not draw active business income earned abroad into the corporate tax base and that only passive income is taxed in order to capture the income which has been shifted abroad for tax avoidance purposes.

The move towards the taxation of foreign passive income should go hand-in-hand with the introduction of relief against double taxation. Currently, Costa Rica's tax system does not provide for any unilateral double tax relief. As pointed out, only two tax treaties are currently in force. In the short run, Costa Rica should consider introducing unilateral tax relief to prevent double taxation of foreign-source passive income. In the medium run, the country could consider the merits of whether it should strategically expand its tax treaty network in order to negotiate lower withholding tax rates and to provide relief against double taxation.

The costs and benefits of double tax treaties should be weighed carefully. Double tax treaties can bring a range of advantages to a country and to those investing in them, but they need to be carefully designed. The negotiation and implementation of double tax treaties can be complex and can absorb valuable administrative resources. As double tax treaties typically lower withholding tax rates, they could provide a windfall gain for foreign investment already in place in Costa Rica and, therefore, could result in a loss of government tax revenues. Whether a capital importing country benefits from signing a double tax treaty will depend largely on whether it realises sufficient gains from increased FDI to offset any tax revenue losses (IMF, 2014). Entering into an increased number of tax treaties would allow Costa Rica also to negotiate lower withholding tax rates levied by other countries on payments made to Costa Rica. This could allow Costa Rica to raise tax revenues from taxing foreign-source passive income and it would provide Costa Rica with the tools to obtain information on the financial activities of its tax residents and their offshore investments. The latter objective can also be achieved through the Convention on Mutual Administrative Assistance in Tax Matters, which Costa Rica has already signed.

The inclusion within tax treaties of provisions that prevent tax treaty abuse is an important instrument to minimise the potential costs and the abuse of tax treaties. The work advanced under Action 6 of the OECD/G20 Base Erosion and Profit Shifting (BEPS) project recognised the importance of preventing the granting of treaty benefits in inappropriate circumstances. A guiding principle is that benefits of a treaty should not be available where the main purpose was just to secure a more favourable tax position. Different techniques to prevent treaty abuse are available including General Anti-Avoidance Rules based on a Principal Purposes Test and specific anti-avoidance rules such as a Limitation on Benefits rule. As a member of the Inclusive Framework on BEPS (see below), Costa Rica has committed to introduce the minimum standard that prevents tax treaty abuse in all of its double tax agreements.

Taxing foreign-source passive income could go hand in hand with the introduction of Controlled-Foreign-Corporation (CFC) rules. CFC rules enable jurisdictions to tax income earned by subsidiaries located in foreign jurisdictions. CFC rules typically apply to passive income which is retained abroad (i.e. interests, dividends, and royalties). As Costa Rica is a high tax country, its domestic companies may face tax-induced incentives to transfer assets, such as intellectual property, to low-tax jurisdictions such that the corresponding income streams escape taxation in Costa Rica. This income would come within the reach of the tax administration with CFC rules. Over time, Costa Rica might therefore want to consider introducing CFC rules.

Costa Rica should consider introducing additional tax base protection measures. For instance, the current CIT system does not foresee a limit on the amount of expenses incurred to earn foreign-source passive income which are deductible from the Costa Rican CIT base. Government may want to ensure that costs incurred to earn foreign-source passive income are only deductible from the Costa Rican foreign-source passive income tax base.

The current tax reform proposal maintains the country's territorial tax system but includes foreign-source passive income within the CIT base. Dividends, interest and royalties that arise from the company's foreign "profitable activities" seem to escape from taxation, however. This would imply that the tax base is not broadened significantly; moreover, it would result in high administrative costs to prevent that income from "non-profitable activities" is re-characterised to escape taxation. Also the tax rate has not been set. The tax reform proposal does introduce unilateral double tax relief; companies would be entitled to a tax credit equal to the minimum of the foreign tax effectively paid or 15% of foreign-source taxable passive income.

High taxes on dividends makes Costa Rica not a very attractive location for FDI

Effective Tax Rates on FDI show the combined impact of the CIT and withholding taxes on foreign direct investment in Costa Rica. Box 2.1 discussed EATRs and EMTRs for investments in different assets and by different types of domestic firms under various financing arrangements. However, these results only capture effective taxation on domestic investments, corresponding to the assumption that both the investor and the company are residents of Costa Rica. Modelling effective taxation on activities of foreign subsidiaries of MNEs implies that, in addition to standard domestic tax features, taxes on cross-border flows of income as well as interactions between tax systems in source and residence countries have to be accounted for.

ETR calculations have to incorporate the reduced withholding tax rates as set in tax treaties. While countries typically define a set of standard withholding tax rates on international payments of dividends, interest and royalties in their domestic tax codes, bilateral tax treaties are concluded to reduce or eliminate double taxation. To achieve this, treaties often include a reciprocal reduction in withholding tax rates as well as provisions for double tax relief at the level of the recipient (located in the residence country), such as foreign tax credits or dividend participation exemptions. As a result, outgoing income flows are typically subject to different tax rates depending on the location of the foreign investor. Conversely, incoming income flows may receive different tax treatment in the residence country due to the fact that they originated from different source countries. Effective taxation on in- and out-flows of FDI therefore varies across country pairs, implying that country-level analyses become considerably more complex.

ETRs on FDI vary significantly across investor countries but are high for FDI in Costa Rica compared to the tax burden on investment in similar countries. Box 2.2 presents results for effective tax rates on inbound FDI, comparing ETRs on investments from a fixed group of investor countries (i.e. where the investing parent company is located) across a set of competing host countries (i.e. where the investment takes place). Investor countries include the main Latin American countries including Argentina, Brazil, Chile, Colombia, Mexico, Peru and Venezuela, as well as the main investor countries from other continents (see Tables 2.4 and 2.5, respectively). The group of host countries is more narrowly defined, including all Central American countries except Belize. In addition, three more countries with similar levels of GDP per capita and FDI are included in this group, namely the Dominican Republic, Ecuador and Uruguay. The high withholding tax rates in Costa Rica and the country's very limited tax treaty network results in high ETRs compared to most other countries in the region which have used the general design of their tax system more actively in attracting FDI.

Strengthening the investment climate in Costa Rica requires reforming the CIT system on different tax fronts. Costa Rica has started tightening its CIT base rules in order to prevent tax avoidance and evasion of MNEs. Such reforms are welcomed and follow international best practices. However, these reforms have to go hand in hand with tax policy reforms and, after careful analysis, the potential expansion of the country's tax treaty network. In general, a country's statutory tax provisions start affecting economic outcomes more strongly when it becomes more difficult for MNEs to strip profits out of a country through transfer mispricing or thin capitalisation. In such an environment of tighter legal tax rules and tax enforcement, Costa Rica's high statutory CIT rate, the relatively high withholding tax rates and the absence of international double tax relief become more distortive. The lower tax burdens in other LAC countries could exacerbate these effects.

Different corporate tax reform options exist to strengthen the investment climate. Costa Rica could lower its standard CIT rate, although the fiscal costs of doing so mean that this would most likely need to occur gradually; it could lower its standard withholdings tax rates or lower withholding tax rates for a selection of countries through the strategic expansion of its tax treaty network. These different tax policy options vary in their economic advantages and costs. A broader corporate tax rate reduction and/ or a general reduction in withholding tax rates would more strongly stimulate investment across the board, but would also result in larger windfall gains for current investors and entail larger tax revenue losses; the latter is an important consideration in light of Costa Rica's urgent need to balance its budget deficit.

Locational decisions of foreign investments are determined by a wide variety of factors. Strengthening the investment climate requires an in-depth evaluation of how the domestic and foreign investment climate in Costa Rica could be strengthened. The factors that have contributed to FDI inflows into Costa Rica in the past may not necessarily be sufficient to continue attracting high amounts of FDI in the future. Although Costa Rica is recognised for being an attractive business location because of its skilled labour force, the country's political stability and its geographical location, the country would nevertheless benefit from a whole-of-government evaluation of its investment climate. Such an analysis would include an evaluation of the corporate tax system including its wide-range system of tax incentives; such an analysis would also take into account the tax system in the investor's country of tax residence, and in particular whether Costa Rica's trading partners and investor countries operate a worldwide or territorial tax system and the type of double tax relief they provide. Such an evaluation could inform an assessment of the impact of specific corporate tax reductions and tax incentives on the overall tax burden faced by foreign investors, and on the incentives to invest in Costa Rica.

Box 2.2. **Effective tax rates on foreign direct investment**

Economic model and assumptions

The modelling approach used to calculate ETRs on domestic investments has been described in Box 2.1. As noted, the analysis of domestic ETRs accounts for tax depreciation schedules as well as elements of personal income taxation affecting shareholder level decisions. In the international context, however, we adopt a simplified approach in order to focus the analysis on the effects of corporate taxation on multinational FDI decisions. The analysis assumes that tax depreciation completely follows economic depreciation and that investors are exempt from personal income taxation, in line with the observation that, in the context of MNEs, larger shares of investors are either not resident in the country of the parent company or institutional investors which are typically tax exempt on dividend income or capital gains.

As before, we calculate EMTRs, EATRs as well as the cost of capital. However, in an international investment context we are most interested in the EATR as it captures the effects of taxation on location decisions; this interpretation is equivalent to the assumption that the MNE expects to earn an economic rent, e.g. by exploiting firm-specific advantages, but will choose to locate production in only one among several possible source countries due to economies of scale. In contrast, the EMTR on international investments captures the incentive faced by MNEs to increase the scale of production in a given source country where production already takes place.

To maintain comparability with the domestic analysis we take the same assumptions as before with regard to the pre-tax rate of return (20%) as well as inflation (3.5%) and real interest rates (12%) in host (i.e. source) countries. These parameters are held constant across host countries in order to isolate the effects of the tax systems on the ETRs. For LAC residence countries we assume the same inflation and real interest rates; however, for residence countries outside the region we assume an inflation rate of only 1.5%, again in line with the 5-year average.

Cross-border income flows are subject to corporate income and withholding taxes in the host country; in the residence country foreign tax relief may be available. However, the tax treatment of foreign source income varies across residence countries and may be altered through treaty provisions. In general, we consider three possible relief methods: exemption, foreign tax credits and deductions. If a residence country has a participation exemption repatriated income is not subject to additional taxation. With foreign tax credits the residence country provides relief for taxes paid in the host country limited to the amount which would be due in case production would have taken place in the country of the parent company. In this case a residence country corporate tax liability may arise only if the corporate tax rate is higher than in the host country. Deductions are the least favourable relief method. In this case recipients in the residence country can deduct foreign taxes paid in the source country from their taxable income, implying that there will in any case be a corporate tax liability.

Box 2.2. **Effective tax rates on foreign direct investment** *(continued)*

Tax treaties aim at reducing double taxation by reducing withholding taxes and potentially providing more generous foreign tax relief. Changes in relief methods, e.g. from credits or deductions to exemption, can have large impacts on bilateral ETRs. The treaty network is thus a crucial element in determining ETRs on inbound FDI in any given host country. Data on tax treaties and related tax parameters are presented in the next subsection.

In line with the theoretical model developed by Devereux and Griffith (1999), we consider a parent company, located in the residence country, undertaking an investment in the host country through a wholly-owned subsidiary. Compared to domestic companies MNEs have access to a wider range of financing arrangements. The parent company can, for instance, provide funds to the subsidiary through internal debt or equity, raising the required funds through retained earnings, external debt or new equity from its shareholders. Following the discussion in Yoo (2003) we limit the number of relevant financing structures to seven:[a] (i) the subsidiary uses retained earnings to finance the investment; the subsidiary raises new equity from the parent and the parent uses (ii) retained earnings, (iii) new equity or (iv) external debt to finance the equity issuance; the subsidiary obtains a loan from the parent uses (v) retained earnings, (vi) new equity or (vii) external debt to finance the equity issuance. However, in the context of international investments we do not offer a separate discussion of the effects of different financing structures on ETRs or possible implications for multinational tax planning.[b] Instead, we construct weighted (or composite) ETRs, using equal weights for each financing structure, so as to produce composite ETRs reflecting the impact of the main tax parameters relevant for international investment decisions.

Empirical results

Effective average tax rates (EATR) on international investments are presented in Tables 2.4 and 2.5. Both tables depict the set of host countries in rows and residence countries in columns. Table 2.4 includes the main regional investor countries as discussed above: Argentina, Brazil, Chile, Colombia, Mexico, Peru and Venezuela. In the case of Costa Rica it shows that the weighted EATR on foreign investments from any of these residence countries is equal to 29.5%.[c] This result is due to the high statutory corporate and withholding tax rates in Costa Rica combined with the fact that residence countries use only indirect foreign tax credits as a relief for taxes paid in host countries; Costa Rica does not have any tax treaties with regional countries. In addition, this result also shows how debt finance by subsidiaries or parent companies can lead to considerably lower EATRs. As discussed above, our composite EATRs are constructed by placing an equal weight on each of the financing structures; however, EATRs under debt finance are low enough to move the composite EATR just below the statutory rate of 30%, despite taking into account the additional withholding taxes; EATRs under equity finance are close to 40%.

Comparing the 29.5% with EATRs on investments in other host countries shows that Costa Rica has the highest EATR among the set of selected peer countries (excluding the six larger Latin American countries). Apart from Panama most other neighbouring countries in Central America do not have extensive treaty networks; the results are thus driven by statutory corporate and withholding tax rates, implying that Costa Rica ranks comparatively high with regard to EATRs from regional investor countries. The other three peer countries, the Dominican Republic, Ecuador and Uruguay, have developed larger treaty networks, allowing them to improve investment conditions to and from selected regional or non-regional countries. Among them, Ecuador offers the most generous conditions to regional investors, for example, through the use of participation exemptions, a combination of low withholding tax rates and favourable treatment of foreign source income implies that composite EATRs on investments in Ecuador are reduced to 10.9% and 13.9% for investments from Colombia and Peru, respectively.

Box 2.2. **Effective tax rates on foreign direct investment** *(continued)*

Table 2.4. **Effective average tax rates on investments from Central and Latin American countries**

	Latin American and Caribbean investor countries						
	Argentina	Brazil	Chile	Colombia	Mexico	Peru	Venezuela
Costa Rica	29.5	29.5	29.5	29.5	29.5	29.5	29.5
El Salvador	25.7	25.1	24.7	29.2	24.7	24.7	25.1
Guatemala	25.5	24.8	21.2	28.9	22.0	22.0	24.8
Honduras	27.1	27.1	27.1	29.2	27.1	27.1	27.1
Nicaragua	25.9	25.9	25.9	29.2	25.9	25.9	25.9
Panama	25.5	24.8	23.8	28.9	22.0	23.8	24.8
Dominican Rep.	25.6	25.1	25.1	29.0	25.1	25.1	25.1
Ecuador	25.4	16.3	17.7	10.9	21.9	13.9	24.7
Uruguay	25.5	24.8	22.2	28.9	22.0	22.2	24.8
Argentina	-	30.8	30.5	30.5	32.0	32.0	30.8
Brazil	19.3	-	25.3	29.4	25.3	25.3	25.3
Chile	25.4	24.7	-	28.9	22.0	23.1	42.3
Colombia	33.8	33.8	33.8	-	33.8	29.3	33.8
Mexico	27.1	27.1	24.7	29.2	-	27.1	27.4
Peru	25.6	24.9	21.5	21.2	24.2	-	24.9

Source: Authors' calculations based on OECD ETR Model.

The lower part of Table 2.4 shows composite EATRs for investments in larger Latin American economies. Although these countries have developed extensive treaty networks, they also tend to maintain relatively high statutory corporate and withholding tax rates. As a result, EATRs on investments from regional countries are comparatively high, sometimes exceeding the EATR on investments in Costa Rica. However, these economies are larger and more diversified, and provide a better qualified labour force as well as public infrastructure, thus making them a more attractive target for foreign investment than Costa Rica.

Table 2.5 shows the composite EATRs on investments from selected non-regional countries to the same set of source countries. EATRs are generally lower than in Table 2.4. A part of this effect is due to the assumption, in line with observed 5-year averages, that inflation is around 2 percentage points lower in European and North American investor countries. As discussed in the context of domestic investments, corporate tax is levied on nominal returns and lower inflation thus reduces effective taxation. EATRs on investments from non-regional residence countries are thus generally somewhat lower than the rates depicted in Table 2.4.

As before the EATRs on investment into Costa Rica are among the highest in the region, with the exception of Spain and Germany, the two countries with which Costa Rica has signed bilateral tax treaties. In both cases the treaty provides a reduction in withholding tax rates for outbound payments from 15% to 5% as well as a full participation exemption in the country of the recipient. The combined effect of these two provisions is equal to a reduction in the composite EATR of approximately 5 percentage points. Comparing EATRs across host countries confirms the result that, in the absence of bilateral tax treaties, EATRs on investments into Costa Rica are among the highest in the region. However, these results also highlight how other regional countries make use of their treaty networks to selectively reduce EATRs.

Box 2.2. **Effective tax rates on foreign direct investment** *(continued)*

Panama, for instance, has treaties with the Netherlands, Spain and the UK which fully eliminate withholding taxes on dividend payments to those countries. Ecuador and Uruguay also provide treaty benefits for several of the regional as well as non-regional investor countries, although in most cases reduced rates remain above zero.

Larger Latin American economies have developed a much denser network of bilateral tax treaties. As depicted in Table 2.1, Mexico currently has 56 treaties while Brazil and Chile both have more than 30. A more active tax treaty policy allows these countries to improve investment conditions with selected investor countries, potentially in line with general economic and trade policy considerations. As a consequence, composite EATRs on investments into these countries, depicted in the lower part of Table 2.5, show much more variation across investor countries. While investments from non-treaty countries into one of these large economies tends to be subject to relatively high EATRs, extensive treaty networks imply that investments from the selected group of non-regional countries are mostly taxed at much lower effective rates. Investments from non-treaty countries into Argentina, for instance, are subject to EATRs of just above 30% (e.g. see Table 2.4); however, investments from low-inflation countries where treaties exist are subject to rates well below 20% (see Table 2.5).

Table 2.5. **Effective average tax rates on investments from non-regional countries**

	Other investor countries								
	Belgium	**Canada**	**Germany**	**Italy**	**Netherlands**	**Spain**	**Switzerland**	**UK**	**US**
Costa Rica	18.8	18.9	13.7	18.9	18.9	13.7	17.3	18.9	18.8
El Salvador	13.7	13.7	13.7	13.7	13.7	11.1	13.4	13.8	17.7
Guatemala	10.2	10.1	10.1	10.2	10.1	10.1	7.2	10.1	17.6
Honduras	16.3	16.3	16.3	16.3	16.3	16.3	13.4	16.3	17.7
Nicaragua	15.0	15.0	15.0	15.0	15.0	15.0	11.5	15.0	17.7
Panama	12.9	12.9	12.8	12.8	7.3	7.3	10.6	7.3	17.6
Dominican Rep.	14.2	14.2	14.2	14.2	14.2	8.8	11.4	14.3	17.6
Ecuador	5.0	8.5	5.3	5.3	7.2	5.0	2.1	5.6	17.5
Uruguay	11.3	11.2	10.1	11.2	11.2	7.3	7.2	11.2	17.6
Argentina	19.7	19.7	19.7	19.7	19.8	19.8	17.4	19.8	19.7
Brazil	14.2	14.2	14.2	14.2	14.2	14.2	12.6	14.2	17.8
Chile	6.9	12.2	33.8	33.5	35.1	9.4	13.4	9.4	32.5
Colombia	23.2	23.2	23.2	23.2	23.2	23.2	20.3	23.2	23.1
Mexico	13.7	13.7	13.7	16.3	11.1	13.7	8.3	11.2	17.7
Peru	13.2	13.2	13.2	13.2	14.5	14.5	11.6	15.9	17.6

Source: Authors' calculations based on OECD ETR Model.

Notes: a. Note that since we are excluding personal income taxation from this analysis the number of relevant financing structures actually reduces to five: retained earnings finance by the subsidiary as well as debt or equity finance at subsidiary and parent levels.

b. However, the full set of results is available from the authors on request.

c. The calculations assume that a Costa Rican non-listed subsidiary makes dividend payments to a parent company in another jurisdiction, which implies that a 15% withholding tax rate applies.

Costa Rica provides a wide range of corporate tax incentives

Costa Rica provides a wide range of corporate tax incentives, including an indirect tax relief for the tourism and agricultural sector, a FTZ regime and tax subsidies for not-for-profit organisations. Some of these tax incentives lack transparency and the requirements that need to be fulfilled to qualify for them are not always straightforward. The system has created opportunities for aggressive tax planning and has put CIT revenues under pressure. As part of its tax reform, government is planning to reassess its current system of corporate tax incentives with the aim of streamlining the incentives and increasing transparency. The OECD welcomes this reform.

Costa Rica has a FTZ regime which offers a wide range of tax incentives.[2] The regime exempts profits from CIT, provides for import duty exemptions and exemptions from local taxation. In general, the FTZ regime exempts profits from CIT for 8 years and provides a 50% CIT reduction during the following 4 years, but differences exist depending on the types of activities and the location of the FTZ (see Table 2.6). Profits from the sale to the domestic market are taxed under separate tax rules.

Table 2.6. **General benefits offered to most companies operating under the FTZ regime**

	Within GAMA*	Outside GAMA
Benefits	CIT exemption for 8 years	CIT exemption for 12 years
	Plus, 4 extra years subject to 50% of CIT	Plus, 6 extra years subject to 50% of CIT
	Plus, in total 10 year exemptions from real estate tax, immovable property transfer tax, from the business license fee and all taxes on remittances abroad. VAT exemption on some public services. Right to a bonus equivalent to 10% of the amount paid for salaries in the previous year after deduction SSC	

*GAMA: Gran Area Metropolitana Ampliada.

Free Trade Zone regimes are common in the LAC region. Many countries in the region implement direct and/or indirect tax incentives for FDI; this often includes CIT reductions or exemptions for a significant length of time. In addition to Costa Rica, FTZ regimes can be found in, for instance, Colombia, the Dominican Republic, Nicaragua, Honduras, Mexico, Puerto Rico, Chile, and Paraguay.

The FTZ tax regime does not lower the effective tax burden on investment from regional countries into Costa Rica (see Table 2.7) if the return is paid directly to the foreign parent company in the form of dividends or interest. Although the FTZ regime in Costa Rica does lower the tax burden on investment in Costa Rica, it does imply that the investor's residence country will be able to raise more tax revenues (as it will have to provide lower foreign tax credits) on the return on investment which is paid directly to the parent company in the country of residence (and not to a related entity located in a third country or by engaging in tax strategies that allow benefiting from tax deferral). Overall, the tax burden on FDI into a FTZ is only slightly lower than the tax burden on FDI in the regular economy of Costa Rica. A similar conclusion emerges for the FTZ regimes in other regional countries; they do lower the tax burden in the host country but they allow the residence country to raise higher tax revenues. FTZ tax competition amongst LAC countries is particularly detrimental to the smaller LAC countries and/ or the countries that do not tax foreign sourced income, such as Costa Rica.

The FTZ tax regime does, however, significantly reduce the tax burden on FDI from non-regional countries into Costa Rica as many of the non-regional investor countries provide participation exemptions. EATRs can even become negative as the parent company might be able to benefit from interest deductibility in the home country if it borrows to finance an investment in a FTZ regime in Costa Rica.

While the FTZ regime might have brought economic advantages to the country, it remains important to regularly assess the actual cost and benefits of the FTZ regime. Such ongoing analysis could be supported by an in-depth evaluation of the methodology that is currently applied to weigh the costs and benefits of the FTZ regime to ensure that this approach is consistent with international best practice. Cost-benefit analyses should focus on the additional investment, employment and productivity generated by the FTZ regime. They should also take into account the relatively high tax burden imposed by the regular tax system, which may discourage domestic investment, as well as the tax-induced distortions in market competition between companies within and outside of the FTZs. The evaluation would also take into account the tax incentives offered by other LAC countries. This type of comprehensive analysis would allow the costs and benefits of the FTZ regime to be regularly assessed and changes and/or improvements made to the system as and when appropriate.

In order to comply with WTO rules, certain companies located in an FTZ are allowed to sell goods and services to the domestic economy; certain restrictions to the amount of sales might apply. Profits that are earned on the sales to the domestic market are typically taxed at the standard CIT rate. Trade between the domestic economy and the FTZ regime creates tax evasion opportunities as businesses with a subsidiary in both the regular domestic economy and the FTZ might try to transfer as much profits as possible to their FTZ subsidiary. Transfer pricing rules should be applied and enforced in relation to companies in the FTZs.

Box 2.3. **Effective tax rates on FDI in free trade zones**

As highlighted in the main text, several regional countries introduced free trade zones in order to stimulate foreign direct investment. In contrast to bilateral tax treaties, free trade zones provide tax incentives for foreign investment irrespective of the location of parent companies or ultimate shareholders. While free trade zones typically offer benefits with regard to several different taxes, the following calculations focus only on corporate tax incentives available through FTZs in Costa Rica, El Salvador, Colombia, Mexico and the Dominican Republic.

As shown in Table 2.7, the free trade zones in Costa Rica, El Salvador and the Dominican Republic offer an initial exemption of 100% of the profits generated within the zones, subject to specific time limits; benefits may be extended for multiple periods or else the share of exempted profits is gradually reduced. While the Dominican Republic continues to tax dividend payments from companies located in the FTZ, Costa Rica and El Salvador exempt these types of payments. In Colombia profits generated within the FTZ are subject to a preferential corporate tax rate of 20% and dividends continue to be taxed at the applicable rates. Mexico, on the other hand, provides no preferential rate, but exempts dividend payments originating in the FTZ from withholding taxes.

Box 2.3. **Effective tax rates on FDI in free trade zones** *(continued)*

Table 2.7. **EATRs on investments from regional countries into free trade zones**

	FTZ: Latin American and Caribbean investor countries						
	Argentina	Brazil	Chile	Colombia	Mexico	Peru	Venezuela
Costa Rica	24.8	24.1	17.0	28.3	21.2	21.2	24.1
El Salvador	24.8	24.1	17.0	28.3	21.2	21.2	24.1
Dominican Rep.	24.8	24.1	17.0	28.3	21.2	21.2	24.1
Colombia	25.3	24.6	20.4	-	21.8	15.8	24.6
Mexico	25.7	25.1	22.3	29.2	-	22.3	25.4

Source: Authors' calculations based on OECD ETR Model.

EATRs on investments within the FTZs of the respective source countries are summarised in Tables 2.7 and 2.8. As expected, the EATRs on investments into Costa Rica, El Salvador and the Dominican Republic do not vary across investor countries because in the absence of participation exemptions effective taxation is determined by CIT rates in the residence countries (Table 2.7). Comparing the results with the EATRs in Table 2.5 shows that the overall reductions in effective taxation due to the FTZs are limited, particularly for investments from countries with relatively high CIT rates such as, for instance, Argentina, Brazil, Colombia and Venezuela. For investments from these countries into Costa Rica the EATRs decrease by only between 1 and 5 percentage points, in line with the fact fewer foreign tax credits can now be claimed in the residence countries (i.e. tax revenues are shifted from source to residence countries). However, the case of Chile shows that FTZs have stronger effects on the EATR when CIT rates are considerably lower in residence countries (12.5 percentage points for Costa Rica). As expected, the effects of the FTZs in Mexico and Colombia are lower; however, the participation exemption for dividend payments from Colombia to Peru now has a more significant effect.

Table 2.8. **EATRs on investments from non-regional countries into free trade zones**

	FTZ: other investor countries								
	Belgium	Canada	Germany	Italy	Netherlands	Spain	Switzerland	UK	US
Costa Rica	-10.5	8.3	-10.6	-10.6	7.0	-11.7	-13.3	-11.7	17.4
El Salvador	-10.5	8.3	-10.6	-10.6	7.0	-11.7	-12.0	-11.7	17.4
Dominican Rep.	-3.4	8.3	-3.5	-3.4	7.0	-11.7	-7.1	-4.2	17.4
Colombia	9.6	9.4	9.5	9.5	9.4	9.4	6.5	9.5	17.5
Mexico	11.2	11.1	11.1	11.2	11.1	11.1	8.3	11.2	17.7

Source: Authors' calculations based on OECD ETR Model.

A different picture emerges from Table 2.8. Since many of the non-regional investor countries provide participation exemptions, i.e. Belgium, Germany, Italy, Spain, Switzerland and the UK, the effects of the free trade zones are much more pronounced. In these cases EATRs on debt-financed investments turn negative because parent companies benefit from interest deductibility although they do not have a tax liability in their country of residence; for residence countries with participation exemptions this effect is strong enough to yield negative composite EATRs. As before, the EATRs for Costa Rica and El Salvador are the same for investors from a given residence country; however, the EATR for investments into the

Box 2.3. **Effective tax rates on FDI in free trade zones** *(continued)*

Dominican Republic is now somewhat higher due to the withholding tax on dividends which is still levied. If tax relief is provided in the form of foreign tax credits, the effects of the free trade zones are again stronger for investments originating in countries with lower corporate income tax rates, such as Canada and the Netherlands. Investments from the US, on the other hand, still face approximately the same EATRs due to the comparatively high statutory corporate income tax rate in the country of residence.

Costa Rica needs to make further progress on addressing Base Erosion and Profit Shifting (BEPS)[3]

Protecting domestic tax bases against international tax avoidance and evasion is a priority. Domestic tax base erosion and profit shifting arises when businesses can exploit gaps and mismatches between different countries' tax systems; BEPS negatively affects tax revenues as well as the efficiency and the ability of tax systems to create a level playing field for all firms. While BEPS is a worldwide concern, it is of particular importance to developing and emerging economies where tax legislation and its administration may struggle with the complexities of modern business. Furthermore, Costa Rica's high CIT rate places it at particular risk of tax avoidance and hence, of revenue losses. In the absence of effective anti-avoidance measures, MNEs investing in Costa Rica may be able to obtain substantial tax advantages by engaging in BEPS strategies to shift profits out of the country. To prevent such tax planning and enable the collection of a fair share of tax on host country profits from such enterprises, Costa Rica should strengthen its tax base protection rules.

Costa Rica has agreed to implement all four minimum standards and recently established a BEPS Commission. Costa Rica has actively participated in the OECD/G20 BEPS project. To ensure a consistent global approach to the implementation of the OECD/G20 BEPS project, OECD and G20 countries have developed the Inclusive Framework on BEPS (IF) which allows interested countries and jurisdictions to work on an equal footing with OECD and G20 members on developing standards on BEPS related issues and reviewing and monitoring the implementation of the whole BEPS package. The first meeting of the inclusive framework took place in June and July 2016, and Costa Rica participated and agreed to the implementation of the four minimum standards. In August 2016, Costa Rican tax authorities established a BEPS Commission to work on a domestic regulatory framework to implement the BEPS Action Plan.

All countries participating in the IF are expected to implement the four minimum standards and implementation will be subject to peer review. The four minimum standards relate to: harmful tax practices (Action 5) (OECD, 2015b); preventing tax treaty abuse (Action 6) (OECD, 2015e); Country-by-Country Reporting (Action 13) (OECD, 2015c); and dispute resolution mechanisms (Action 14) (OECD, 2015d). A robust process for peer review assessment of all countries' implementation of the BEPS minimum standards is being developed by the IF.

Box 2.4. **A comprehensive package of measures to address BEPS**

The OECD/G20 BEPS project produced a 15-point Action Plan including minimum standards, common approaches, best practices and new guidance in the main policy areas.

- Minimum standards have been agreed upon in the areas of fighting harmful tax practices (Action 5), preventing treaty abuse (Action 6), Country-by-Country Reporting (Action 13) and improving dispute resolution (Action 14). All participating countries are expected to implement these minimum standards and implementation will be subject to peer review.
- A common approach, which will facilitate the convergence of national practices by interested countries, has been outlined to limit base erosion through interest expenses (Action 4) and to neutralise hybrid mismatches (Action 2). Best practices for countries which seek to strengthen their domestic legislation are provided on the building blocks for effective controlled foreign company (CFC) rules (Action 3) and mandatory disclosure by taxpayers of aggressive or abusive transactions, arrangements or structures (Action 12).
- The permanent establishment (PE) definition in the OECD Model Tax Convention has been changed to restrict inappropriate avoidance of tax nexus through commissionaire arrangements or exploitation of specific exceptions (Action 7). Follow-up work is being undertaken in 2016 which will also provide further guidance on the attribution of profits to PEs. In terms of transfer pricing, important clarifications have been made with regard to delineating the actual transaction, and the treatment of risk and intangibles. More guidance has been provided on several other issues to ensure that transfer pricing outcomes are aligned with value creation (Actions 8-10).
- The changes to the PE definition, the clarifications on transfer pricing, and the guidance on CFC rules are expected to substantially address the BEPS risks exacerbated by the digital economy. Several other options, including a new nexus in the form of a significant economic presence, were considered, but not recommended at this stage given the other recommendations plus Value Added Taxes (VAT) will now be levied effectively in the market country facilitating VAT collection (Action 1).
- A multilateral instrument will be implemented to facilitate the modification of bilateral tax treaties (Action 15). The modifications made to existing treaties will address the minimum standards against treaty abuse as well as the updated PE definition.

At the February 2016 G20 Finance Ministers meeting, the inclusive framework for the global implementation of the BEPS project was endorsed, with a reiteration of the commitment to timely implementation of the BEPS project and to continue monitoring and addressing BEPS-related issues for a consistent global approach. Costa Rica is a member of the Inclusive Framework on BEPS.

The tax policy recommendations that can be drawn from this analysis are as follows:

Recommendations

- Simplify the tax depreciation scheme by grouping assets in broad asset classes.
- Address the debt-equity bias, preferably by increasing the withholding tax rates on interest payments to at least the level of dividends, but preferably higher.
- Over time, consider levying taxes on capital income at the individual level and lower the standard CIT rate.
- Introduce a profit-based interest limitation rule, as foreseen in the tax reform proposal.
- Tax all capital gains, both habitual and non-habitual, under the CIT as planned.
- Apply clear and transparent definitions of territoriality.
- Introduce tax relief for the withholding taxes paid on foreign source passive income.
- Ensure that business costs incurred to earn foreign-source passive income can only be deducted from that source of income and not from domestic business income.
- Implement the BEPS OECD/G20 minimum standards.
- Consider the merits of whether to strategically expand Costa Rica's tax treaty network.
- Perform an in-depth cost-benefit analysis of the corporate tax incentives, including the Free Trade Zone regime.

Notes

1. E.g. DGT-R-032-2014 of August 6, 2014; DGT-755-2008 of November 21, 2008; DGT-066-2008 of January 21, 2016

2. Costa Rica is a member of the Inclusive Framework on BEPS. As part of the Inclusive Framework's peer review process, Costa Rica's Free Trade Zone regime is being reviewed by the Forum on Harmful Tax Practices (FHTP) to assess its compliance with the minimum standard developed as part of the work carried out under Action 5 of the BEPS Project. This Tax Policy Review has not involved an assessment of Costa Rica's compliance with the minimum standard and nothing in this report should be taken to prejudge the FHTP's assessment.

3. This paper does not carry out a thorough analysis of the extent to which Costa Rica has effectively implemented the minimum standards of the BEPS package. A robust process for peer review assessment of all countries' implementation of the BEPS minimum standards is being developed by the Inclusive Framework on BEPS, which is the appropriate forum through which such an assessment will be undertaken.

References

Artana, D. and I. Templado (2015), "La eficacia de los incentivos fiscales. El caso de las zonas francas de exportación de Costa Rica, El Salvador, y República Dominicana", [The effectiveness of tax incentives. The case of the export free trade zones of Costa Rica, El Salvador and the Dominican Republic], Interamerican Development Bank, IDB-DP-377.

Bachas, P. and M. Soto (2016), "Not (ch) your average tax system: corporate taxation under weak enforcement", Working Paper, https://www8.gsb.columbia.edu/faculty-research/sites/faculty-research/files/finance/Applied%20Microeconomics/Fall%202016/Corporate_tax_elasticity_BachasSoto_2016%20(1).pdf.

Brys, B., S. Perret, A. Thomas and P. O'Reilly (2016), "Tax Design for Inclusive Economic Growth", *OECD Taxation Working Papers*, No. 26, OECD Publishing, Paris, http://dx.doi.org/10.1787/5jlv74ggk0g7-en.

Carrillo, P., D. Pomeranz and M. Singhal (2014), "Dodging the taxman: firm misreporting and limits to tax enforcement", *Harvard Business School Working Papers* 15-026.

Cnossen, S. (1996), "Company taxes in the European Union: criteria and options for reform", *Fiscal Studies*, Vol. 17, No. 4, pp. 67-97.

de Mooij, R. and M. Devereux (2011), "An Applied Analysis of ACE and CBIT Reforms in the EU", International Tax and Public Finances, 10.1007/s10797-010-9138-8.

Faria, A. (1995), "Source Versus Residence Principle", in *Tax Policy Handbook,* International Monetary Fund, Washington, DC.

Hajkova, D., et al. (2006), "Taxation, business environment and FDI location in OECD countries", *OECD Economics Department Working Papers*, No. 502, OECD Publishing, Paris, http://dx.doi.org/10.1787/874058477248.

Hanappi, T. (Forthcoming), "Loss carry over provisions: measuring effects on tax symmetry and automatic stabilisation", *OECD Taxation Working Papers*, OECD Publishing, Paris.

Harding, M. (2013), "Taxation of dividend, interest, and capital gain income", *OECD Taxation Working Papers,* No. 19, OECD Publishing, Paris, http://dx.doi.org/10.1787/5k3wh96w246k-en.

Hellerstein, W. (2009), "Jurisdiction to impose and enforce income and consumption taxes: towards a unified conception of nexus in value added tax and direct tax: similarities and differences", IBFD, The Netherlands.

IADB (2013), *More than Revenue. Taxation as a Development Tool*, Interamerican Development Bank.

IMF (2014), "Spillovers in international corporate taxation", *IMF Policy Paper*, www.imf.org/external/pp/ppindex.aspx.

Kleven, H., M. Knudsen, K. Kreiner, S. Pedersen and E. Sanz (2011), "Unwilling or unable to cheat: evidence from a tax audit experiment in Denmark", *Econometrica*, Vol. 79 (No. 3), pp. 651-692.

Largaespada, M. (2014), "Nicaragua, tercer país donde más invierten los ticos", [Nicaragua, the third country where costaricans invest the most], *El Nuevo Diario*,

13 February 2014, www.elnuevodiario.com.ni/nacionales/311057-nicaragua-tercer-pais-donde-mas-invierten-ticos/ (accessed 13 February 2017).

OECD (2015a), *Taxation of SMEs in OECD and G20 Countries*, OECD Publishing, Paris, http://dx.doi.org/10.1787/9789264243507-en.

OECD (2015b), *Countering Harmful Tax Practices More Effectively, Taking into Account Transparency and Substance, Action 5 – 2015 Final Report*, OECD Publishing, Paris, http://dx.doi.org/10.1787/9789264241190-en.

OECD (2015c), *Transfer Pricing Documentation and Country-by-Country Reporting, Action 13 – 2015 Final Report*, OECD Publishing, Paris, http://dx.doi.org/10.1787/9789264241480-en.

OECD (2015d), *Making Dispute Resolution Mechanisms More Effective, Action 14 – 2015 final report*, OECD Publishing, Paris, http://dx.doi.org/10.1787/9789264241633-en.

OECD (2015e), *Preventing the Granting of Treaty Benefits in Inappropriate Circumstances, Action 6 – 2015 Final Report*, OECD Publishing, Paris, http://dx.doi.org/10.1787/9789264241695-en.

OECD (2015f), *Limiting Base Erosion Involving Interest Deductions and other Financial Payments, Action 4 – 2015 final report*, OECD Publishing, Paris, http://dx.doi.org/10.1787/9789264241176-en.

OECD (2015g), *Neutralising the Effects Of Hybrid Mismatch Arrangements, Action 2 – 2015 Final Report*, OECD Publishing, Paris, http://dx.doi.org/10.1787/9789264241138-en.

OECD (2015h), *Designing Effective Controlled Foreign Company Rules, Action 3 – 2015 Final Report*, OECD Publishing, Paris, http://dx.doi.org/10.1787/9789264241152-en.

OECD (2015i), *Mandatory Disclosure Rules, Action 12 – 2015 Final Report*, OECD Publishing, Paris, http://dx.doi.org/10.1787/9789264241442-en.

OECD (2015j), *Preventing the Artificial Avoidance of Permanent Establishment Status, Action 7 – 2015 Final Report*, OECD Publishing, Paris, http://dx.doi.org/10.1787/9789264241220-en.

OECD (2015k), *Aligning transfer pricing outcomes with value creation, Actions 8-10 – 2015 Final Report*, OECD Publishing, Paris, http://dx.doi.org/10.1787/9789264241244-en.

OECD (2015l), *Addressing the tax challenges of the digital economy, Action 1 – 2015 Final Report*, OECD Publishing, Paris, http://dx.doi.org/10.1787/9789264241046-en.

OECD (2015m), *Developing a multilateral instrument to modify bilateral tax treaties, Action 15 – 2015 Final Report*, OECD Publishing, Paris, http://dx.doi.org/10.1787/9789264241688-en.

OECD (2015n), *Measuring and monitoring BEPS, Action 11 – 2015 final report*, OECD Publishing, Paris, http://dx.doi.org/10.1787/9789264241343-en.

OECD (2013), *Action Plan on Base Erosion and Profit Shifting*, OECD Publishing, Paris, http://dx.doi.org/10.1787/9789264202719-en.

OECD (2010), *Tax Policy Reform and Economic Growth*, OECD Publishing, Paris, http://dx.doi.org/10.1787/9789264091085-en.

OECD (2009), "Depreciation or consumption of fixed capital", in *Measuring Capital – OECD Manual 2009: Second edition*, OECD Publishing, Paris, http://dx.doi.org/10.1787/9789264068476-8-en.

OECD (2007), *Fundamental Reform of Corporate Income Tax*, OECD Publishing, Paris, http://dx.doi.org/10.1787/9789264038127-en.

OECD (2001), *Corporate Tax Incentives for Foreign Direct Investment*, OECD Publishing, Paris, http://dx.doi.org/10.1787/9789264188402-en.

PROCOMER, COMEX and CINDE (2016), *Balance de las Zonas Francas: Beneficio Neto del Régimen para Costa Rica 2011-2015*, [Balance of free trade zones: net benefit of the regime for Costa Rica 2011-2015].

PWC (2013), "Evolution of territorial tax systems in the OECD", prepared for the Technology CEO Council, www.techceocouncil.org/clientuploads/reports/Report%20on%20Territorial%20Tax%20Systems_20130402b.pdf.

Schon, W. (2010), "Persons and territories: on international allocation of taxing rights", *British Tax Review*, No. 6, pp. 554-562, http://hdl.handle.net/11858/00-001M-0000-0011-3DD4-2.

Tadmore, N. (2007), "Source taxation of cross-border intellectual supplies – concepts, history and evolution into the digital age", *Bulletin for International Taxation*, pp. 2-16.

Van der Schoor, L., A. Saleh and M. Guruswamy (2016), *Incentives Awarded Across Free Zones: Onfirming the Transition to 'Free Zones of the Future?*, https://www.worldfzo.org/AnnualReports/Incentives%20Research%20Paper.pdf.

Zee, H., J. Stotsky and E. Ley (2002), "Tax incentives for business investment: a primer for policy makers in developing countries", *World Development* No. 9, 30, pp. 1497-1516.

Zolt, E. (2015), "Tax incentives: an overview of key concepts and issues", *Capacity Development Programme in International Tax Cooperation*, http://siteresources.worldbank.org/INTTPA/Resources/EassonZoltPaper.pdf.

Chapter 3

Strengthening the role of the personal income tax in Costa Rica

This chapter discusses the design of the personal income tax (PIT) in Costa Rica, including the tax rate schedule and the income threshold where taxpayers start paying tax, the progressivity of the PIT, the PIT withholding system, the schedular PIT design under which different types of labour income are taxed separately and the PIT evasion by liberal professions. The chapter also discusses the design of the social security contributions (SSCs), focusing on the level of the rates and the minimum contribution threshold, as well as their impact on the incentives to work in the formal economy. The chapter discusses the impact of the lack of integration between the PIT and SSC systems. Average and marginal labour income tax wedges show the combined impact of PITs and SSCs on work incentives.

The statistical data for Israel are supplied by and under the responsibility of the relevant Israeli authorities. The use of such data by the OECD is without prejudice to the status of the Golan Heights, East Jerusalem and Israeli settlements in the West Bank under the terms of international law.

Costa Rica relies heavily on SSCs while the PIT plays a limited role

Revenues from social security contributions account for a very large share of total tax revenues. As mentioned in Chapter 1, SSCs accounted for about 34% of Costa Rica's total tax revenues in 2014, which was significantly above the Latin-America and the Caribbean (LAC) average of 16.4% (Figure 3.1). Panama is the only LAC country where SSCs account for a greater share of total tax revenues. The share of SSCs in total tax revenues in Costa Rica is also higher than the OECD average, where SSCs constitute a major source of tax revenues and account on average for around a quarter of total tax revenues.

Figure 3.1. **SSCs as a share of total tax revenues in 2014**

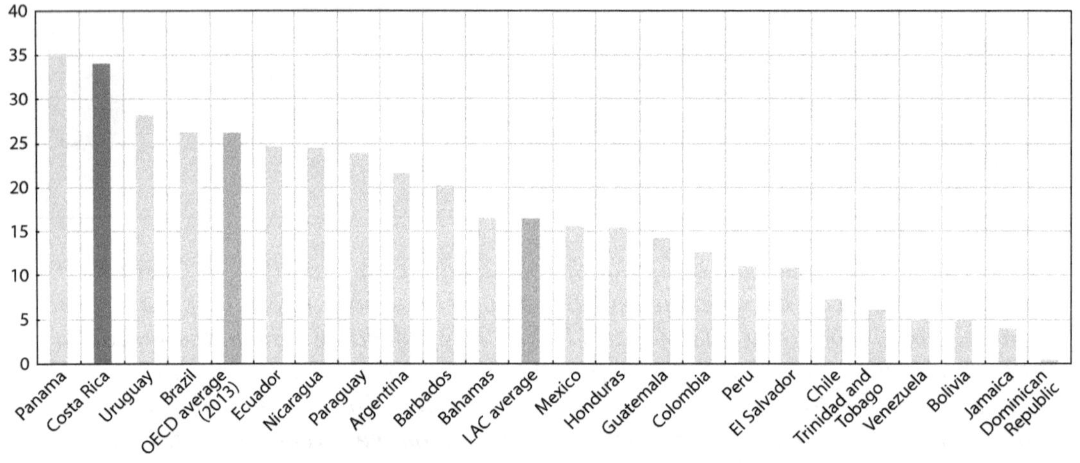

StatLink http://dx.doi.org/10.1787/888933544683

Source: OECD/IDB/CIAT (2016), *Taxing Wages in Latin America and the Caribbean 2016*, OECD Publishing, Paris.

PIT, on the other hand, accounts for a very small share of total tax revenues in Costa Rica. In 2014, PIT revenues amounted to only about 5.8% of total tax revenues. This share is very low in comparison to OECD countries where PIT accounted on average for 24% of total tax revenues in 2014. Costa Rica's revenues from PIT are also low

Figure 3.2. **PIT as a share of total tax revenues in 2014**

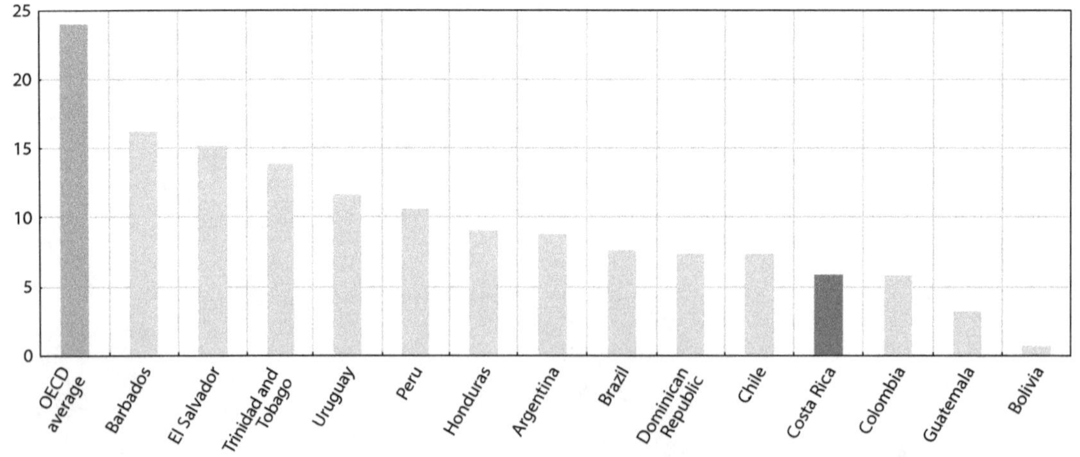

StatLink http://dx.doi.org/10.1787/888933544702

Note: No data was available for Ecuador, Jamaica, Mexico, Nicaragua, Panama, Paraguay and Venezuela.

Source: OECD/IDB/CIAT (2016), *Taxing Wages in Latin America and the Caribbean 2016*, OECD Publishing, Paris.

compared to LAC countries, although low shares of revenues from PIT are a more common characteristic in the region. Many LAC countries collect less than 10% of their total tax revenues from PIT (Figure 3.2).

A large amount of employment income is exempt from PIT, which means that only very few people pay PIT. Costa Rican employees only start paying PIT on earnings exceeding more than 150% of the average wage. Costa Rica's tax-free threshold is high in comparison with LAC countries, where, on average, taxpayers start paying PIT on earnings above a threshold equivalent to 0.99 times the average wage (Figure 3.3). Costa Rica's tax-free threshold is also high compared to common practice in OECD countries where, on average, taxpayers start paying income tax on earnings around one third of the average wage, although considerable differences exist across countries (OECD, 2012). Because of this very high income threshold, only 88 684 people (or close to 2% of the population) were subject to PIT in 2015, significantly eroding potential tax revenues.

Figure 3.3. **Income thresholds at which single individuals start paying income tax, measured as a multiple of the average wage in USD, in 2013**

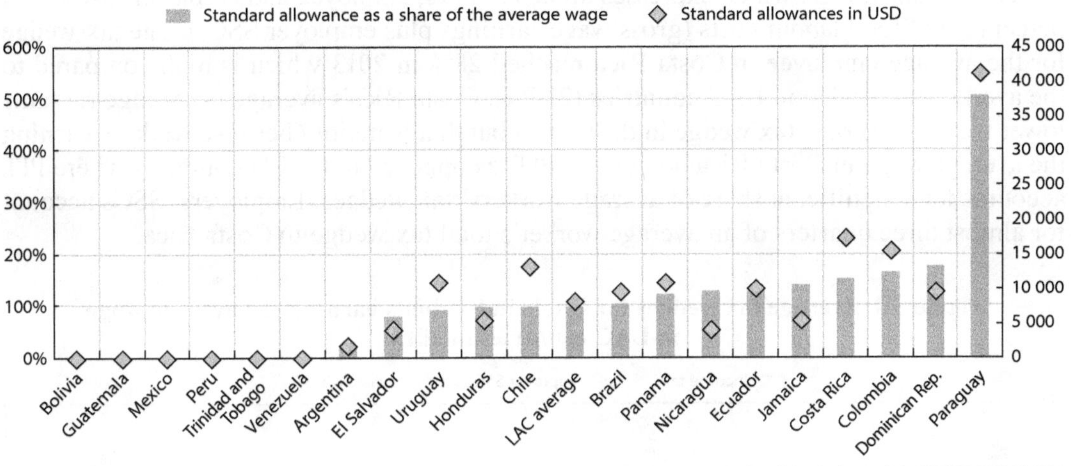

StatLink http://dx.doi.org/10.1787/888933544721

Source: Barreix et al. (2017).

Moreover, personal income tax rates are low. The 2017 PIT rate schedule consists of three tax brackets. The tax rates on employment income range from 0% up to monthly income of CRC 793 000 (EUR 1 320), 10% and 15% on monthly employment income exceeding CRC 1 190 000 (EUR 1 980).

On the other hand, social security contribution rates are high. Costa Rican employees must contribute at a total rate of 9.34% of their monthly gross income. Their contributions are withheld by their employers but, in contrast to most OECD countries, those contributions are not deductible from taxable employment income,[1] which effectively increases the tax burden on employees. In addition, employers' must make contributions equal to 26.33% of the salaries of their employees which they can deduct as costs. Those SSCs cover health and pension contributions paid to the *Caja Costarricence de Seguridad Social* (CCSS), unemployment insurance, family allowances, and contributions for complementary pensions as well as a few additional contributions. Finally, unlike OECD countries, the state also pays for a small share of SSCs (Table 3.1).

Table 3.1. **Social security contribution rates**

	Employee	Employer	State
Old-age pensions	2.84%	5.08%	0.57%
Healthcare	5.50%	9.25%	0.25%
Unemployment insurance		3.00%	
Family allowances (FODESAF)		5.00%	
Popular Bank fee	1.00%	0.50%	
Complementary pensions		1.50%	
National Learning Institute (INA)		1.50%	
Mixed Institute for Social Support (IMAS)		0.50%	
Total	**9.34%**	**26.33%**	**0.82%**

High SSCs – in particular employer SSCs – result in a high average tax burden on labour income. Figure 3.4 compares the tax burden on single workers earning the average wage across LAC countries. The average tax burden on workers is measured as the average tax wedge, which expresses all taxes (PITs, employee and employer SSCs) as a percentage of total labour costs (gross wage earnings plus employer SSCs). The tax wedge for the average employee in Costa Rica reached 28% in 2013 which is high compared to the average tax wedge in LAC countries (21.7%). Costa Rica's average tax wedge remains lower than the average tax wedge in the OECD but that is mainly because workers earning the average wage in Costa Rica do not pay PIT, as opposed to OECD countries where PIT accounts for a significant share of average workers' tax wedges. Employers' SSCs account for almost three quarters of an average worker's total tax wedge in Costa Rica.

Figure 3.4. **Average tax wedges for single individuals earning the average wage in LAC countries in 2013**

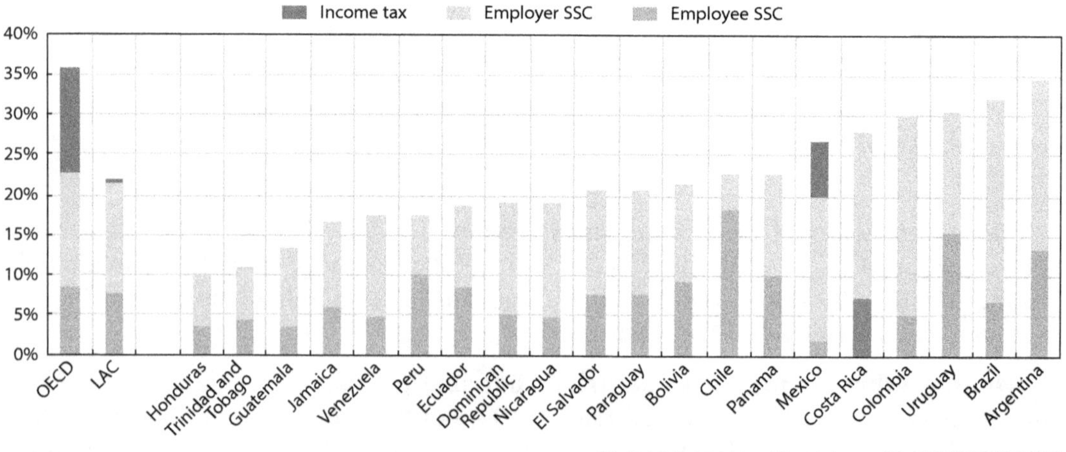

StatLink http://dx.doi.org/10.1787/888933544740

Source: OECD/IDB/CIAT (2016), *Taxing Wages in Latin America and the Caribbean 2016*, OECD Publishing, Paris.

The tax wedge is overall relatively flat but highly regressive at the bottom of the income distribution, which reduces incentives for formalisation

The average tax wedge on labour income is relatively flat. The average tax wedge is about 28% for income between 50% and 170% of the average wage. PIT is paid on income exceeding 170% of the AW. Because of the low PIT rates, the average tax wedge gradually increases to 35% for taxpayers earning five times the average wage (Figure 3.5).

Figure 3.5. **Average tax wedge across earnings levels expressed as a % of the average wage in 2016**

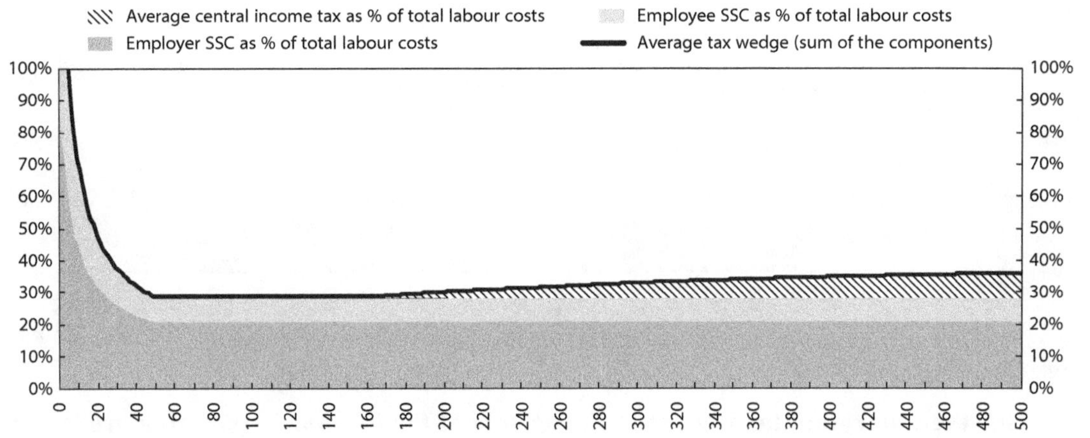

StatLink http://dx.doi.org/10.1787/888933544759

Source: Authors' calculations.

However, the average tax wedge is highly regressive at the bottom of the income distribution. Costa Rica imposes a minimum amount of SSCs if earnings are below a minimum threshold. For workers with earnings below CRC 228 530 per month (about 50% of the average wage in 2016), SSCs that are paid to the CCSS are calculated on the basis of that income threshold irrespective of workers' actual earnings. For other types of contributions, they are calculated on the basis of actual earnings. This minimum contribution makes SSCs under the minimum income threshold regressive – meaning that the average contribution rate is higher for low-income workers. Part-time workers in particular can be subject to very high contribution burdens relative to their earnings. For instance, workers earning 10% of the average wage face an average tax wedge of 68%, which means that they only take home as net pay 32% of what they cost to their employer (Figure 3.5). This minimum contribution is highly distortive as it strongly discourages low-income workers, in particular those working part-time, from joining or remaining in the formal sector.

The minimum contribution base, which makes the average tax wedge regressive at the bottom of the income distribution, has been raised in recent years. Since 2014, the minimum contribution base has been set as a percentage of the minimum wage, increasing over time, and to reach 100% of the minimum wage by October 2019. Raising the minimum contribution base without strengthening compliance with minimum wage legislation and without allowing the minimum base to vary with working hours will further reduce incentives for formal employment, with adverse consequences on both workers and public finances (OECD, forthcoming).

Marginal tax wedges are relatively high due to the combined effect of PITs and SSCs. The marginal tax wedge shows the additional taxes (PIT, employee and employer SSCs) that have to be paid when total labour costs increase with an additional CRC. Taxpayers earning income exceeding 250% of the AW face a marginal tax wedge of about 40%, meaning that 40% of the increase in labour costs is paid to government in the form of taxes and SSCs and only 60% is received by the taxpayer as net-income (Figure 3.6).

Figure 3.6. **Marginal tax wedge across earnings levels expressed as a % of the average wage in 2016**

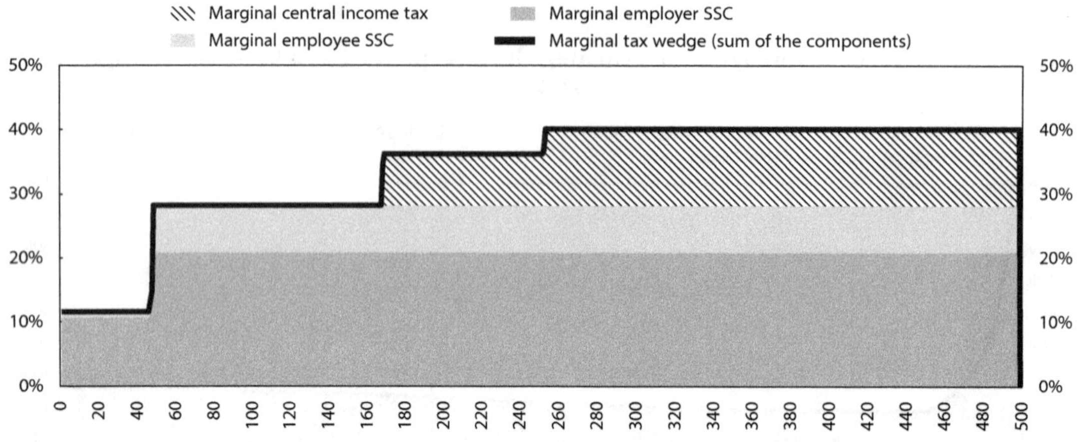

StatLink http://dx.doi.org/10.1787/888933544778

Source: Authors' calculations.

However, marginal tax wedges at the bottom of the income distribution are lower. Figure 3.6 shows that marginal tax wedges at income levels below the SSC minimum earnings threshold are relatively low. If workers earn less than CRC 228 530 per month, the only additional contributions they have to make when they earn an extra CRC amount to 11.6%, because most of their SSCs have already been paid in the form of a lump-sum amount. So, while the minimum SSC threshold discourages workers for participating in the formal labour market, they create an incentive to work more hours for workers who are already in the formal sector because most of their SSCs have already been paid anyway.

In general, high SSCs encourage informality. High labour taxes in the formal sector may push low-productivity workers into the informal sector or unemployment. SSCs increase the cost of employing workers and reduce workers' after-tax earnings. The larger the difference between total labour costs in the formal sector and the return on labour after taxes are deducted, the greater the incentive for both employers and employees to avoid taxes by remaining or joining the informal economy. High levels of informality may in turn negatively affect productivity, growth and trust in government institutions (Box 3.1).

Box 3.1. **Main consequences of informality**

High levels of informality can have significant negative consequences for the economy. First, workers employed in the informal sector have limited access to social protection, inadequate contracts, comparatively lower wages, and are highly vulnerable when they lose their job or when they retire. High levels of informality may also reduce workers' access to training, exacerbating skills shortages. This ultimately generates greater inequalities. This is of particular concern in Latin American countries where inequality is already very high.

The informal sector also affects productivity and growth. Production in the informal sector often generates inefficiencies, either because firms limit their size below their optimal efficiency scale to avoid being detected or because they use outdated production technologies (Andrews et al., 2011). The relative cost advantages enjoyed by informal firms may allow them to stay in business even if they are not productive (Andrews et al., 2011). Firms operating in the informal sector also have a more limited access to finance which constrains investment and to qualified labour.

Box 3.1. **Main consequences of informality** *(continued)*

A significant level of informal economic activity also has significant negative fiscal consequences. High levels of informality reduce the amount of tax revenue received by the government. Many informal workers may also be in receipt of social benefits, adding to the unnecessary fiscal burden on the state. (This is not so clear-cut: it can be argued that taxing the informal sector has limited revenue potential because informal workers and businesses tend to be poor and would entail heavy collection costs).

Finally, high levels of informality, when observed by formal workers, can result in an erosion of trust in public institutions and result in lower tax morale, which may lower revenues through other channels. Importantly, the larger the informal sector, the more incentives people have to remain or become informal (less fear of being sanctioned, view that the informal sector is tolerated).

Recent analysis confirms that taxation, especially through SSCs, has an impact on labour market outcomes. Figure 3.7 (Panel A) shows the relationship across the income distribution between informality and "formalisation costs", proxied by the employee SSCs workers would have to pay to remain or become formal in Costa Rica. This measure can be taken as a lower bound, given that formalisation generally entails additional monetary and non-monetary costs. The white bar identifies the approximate location of the minimum wage. For workers earning above the minimum SSC threshold, this cost is defined as the amount of employee SSCs payable on wages. However, for workers currently excluded from social security programmes, the cost of becoming formal is the amount of SSCs payable at the minimum SSC threshold. As a result, the cost of formalisation will be greater if the shortfall between a worker's income and the established minimum threshold is large. Costa Rica's theoretical costs of formalisation for workers in the lowest income decile (Panel B) are the second highest in LAC after Mexico (OECD, 2016).

Figure 3.7. **Theoretical formality costs as a % of workers' actual wages and informality rates for dependent workers in 2013 (Panel A) and theoretical formality costs for workers in the lowest income decile (Panel B)**

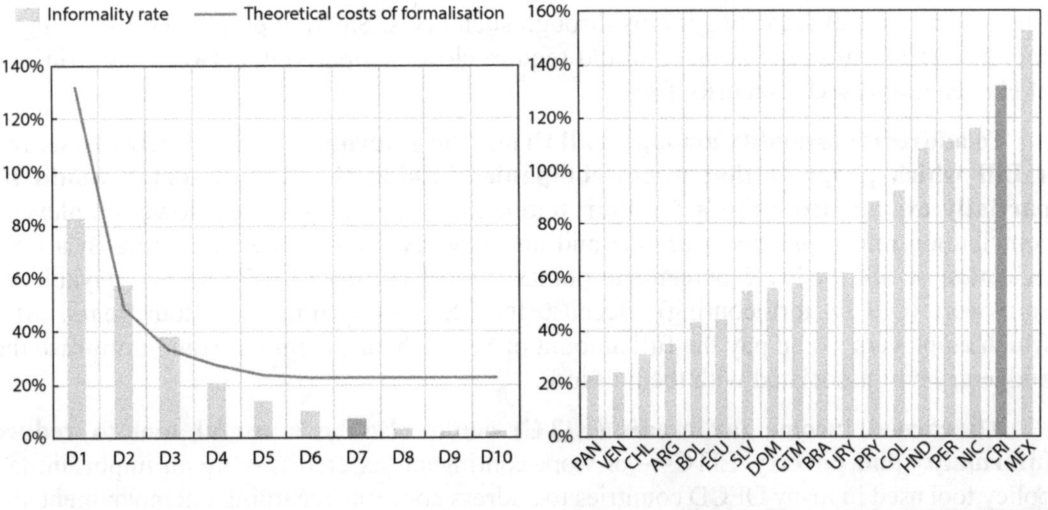

StatLink http://dx.doi.org/10.1787/888933544797

Source: OECD/IDB/CIAT (2016), *Taxing Wages in Latin America and the Caribbean 2016*, OECD Publishing, Paris.

In addition, incentives to pay SSCs are reduced by the universal coverage of core public services, such as health care. Some SSCs are earmarked for benefits associated with the labour market status, in particular pension and unemployment benefits, which can be seen as part of labour compensation. Others, however, finance benefits that are available to all citizens, whether they contribute or not (e.g. training services and child care). Because of this weak link between payments and benefits, incentives to pay into the system and be formal are low.

Reducing SSCs for low-income workers could raise incentives for employers to hire and declare workers and for employees to operate in the formal economy. Lehmann and Muravyev (2012) find evidence, based on a panel of Latin American countries, that a larger tax wedge increases informality and suggest that lowering the tax wedge might be one of the most effective instruments to fight against informality. Such an approach was already adopted to promote formalisation among female domestic workers in Costa Rica. In July 2016, the minimum base which is used as the reference to calculate and charge SSCs was cut in half. Until then, employers who employed part-time domestic workers had a very strong incentive not to declare them to avoid paying a disproportionate amount of SSCs required to ensure their workers.

A better option would be to levy SSCs as a percentage of actual income, which is the common practice in OECD countries. This means that part-time workers would contribute and receive social benefits by making contributions proportional to part-time incomes. Such a measure would avoid penalising low-income workers, would no longer discourage part-time work and would strengthen workers' incentives to work in the formal sector. Levying all SSCs on actual income would also enhance the overall progressivity of the tax and benefit system as low-income workers would contribute less for the benefits that they receive.

Levying SSCs on actual earnings instead of on a minimum threshold or reducing SSCs for low-income workers would nevertheless most likely come at a budgetary cost, which would need to be compensated. To continue ensuring the adequate funding of the social security system, some social benefits – in particular those where there is no clear link between the level of contributions and the level of benefits such as family allowances or health insurance – could be financed through taxes that bear on tax bases other than labour income, including corporate income, consumption or property. Some OECD countries (e.g. France through the *contribution sociale generalisée* – CSG) partly finance their social security systems through such taxes. Shifting part of the financing of social benefits onto general taxes would require close co-operation between the Ministry of Hacienda and social security funds.

To address informality among small firms, the government is currently discussing a Bill which proposes that micro-companies joining the formal sector would be partially exempt from SSCs for four years. The programme would lower employer's contribution rate to health insurance and anti-poverty programmes, resulting in a total reduction of SSCs of 12.5 percentage points, almost cutting in half the rate payable by employers (OECD, forthcoming). Because the SSC cut is limited to four years, after which employers would pay the full amount of SSCs, the programme would minimise the budgetary cost associated with the measure.

An earned income tax credit (EITC) could also be a useful tool to reduce informality and poverty. EITCs – or work-contingent tax credits – are an important tax policy tool used in many OECD countries to address concerns regarding unemployment and inactivity traps. These measures have the dual goal of alleviating poverty and increasing incentives to work, which they achieve by targeting low-income workers (often with children) and imposing some form of work-contingent eligibility rule (Box 3.2). An EITC could be very relevant in the Costa Rican context as it would provide incentives for people to register with the tax authorities to receive the credit and encourage individuals working in informality to put pressure on their employers to become formal (Perry et al., 2007).

Box 3.2. **In-work tax credits**

Work-contingent tax credits or benefits are one of the main measures used in many OECD countries to address concerns regarding unemployment traps and inactivity traps. These measures have the dual motivation of poverty alleviation, and increasing incentives to work. They achieve this by targeting low-income workers (often with children), and imposing some form of work-contingent eligibility rule.

In-work credit schemes are a long established component of the tax-benefit systems in some countries including the UK, US, and have had overall positive effects on employment. Theoretically, in-work credits can have conflicting effects on employment, increasing the incentive to enter employment, but reducing work incentives for those already in employment. However, empirical evidence (based particularly on the US and UK schemes) shows that the overall impact of these schemes on employment is positive.

There are large variations in design across countries, particularly regarding eligibility rules and targeting, credit levels, withdrawal rates and payment methods. Regarding eligibility criteria, countries either require a certain number of hours to be worked each week, or a minimum amount of income to be earned from employment. Additionally, seven countries require the presence of children for eligibility (while the number of children in a family increases the value of credits in six countries). Most countries also target the credit by income level. This is generally achieved by withdrawing the credit as income increases above a certain level. Rates of withdrawal, however, vary significantly. The size of the credit, which is to some extent linked to the withdrawal rate (e.g. large credits tend to be phased out more quickly to limit the fiscal cost), also varies greatly.

Countries have tended to adopt one of three broad approaches:

- High withdrawal rates and generous credits: To maximise the effectiveness of credits at increasing employment (as well as at reducing in-work poverty) a number of countries provide credits at relatively high rates. This is particularly the case in Ireland, the UK, the US, New Zealand, and Belgium where maximum credit payments are all greater than five per cent of the average wage. Ireland in particular is very generous with a maximum credit greater than 20 per cent of the average wage. To reduce fiscal costs, these countries all withdraw these credits at relatively high rates (20 per cent or greater), thereby accepting relatively high marginal effective tax rates (METRs) as a consequence. Ireland is the extreme case with an effective phase-out rate of 60 per cent, emphasising the predominant focus of the Irish FIS on poverty reduction rather than employment goals.
- Low withdrawal rates and smaller credits: Some countries that are more concerned about the negative consequences of high METRs choose to phase out credits over a wider income range, thereby reducing the size of METR increases (but extending the income range facing the increases). However, when limited funding is available this necessarily results in lower credits, which may pose concerns for the effectiveness of the credits at increasing employment and reducing in-work poverty. That said, the lower phase-out rate means they are available to a wider range of workers, potentially providing incentives for some middle-income earners also to move into work or to increase hours worked in order to meet eligibility requirements for the

Box 3.2. **In-work tax credits** *(continued)*

credit. Conversely, this also means that higher METRs are faced by a greater income range, potentially resulting in some workers reducing the number of hours they work. Countries in this category include Canada, France, and Spain (earned income credit).

- Low-to-moderate withdrawal rates and generous credits: Another group of countries also have lower withdrawal rates due to concerns regarding high METRs, but still desire substantial credit amounts in order to achieve a significant work incentive. These countries accept higher fiscal costs in order to achieve this. Denmark, Sweden and the Netherlands are particularly strong examples of this. Concerns in these countries about high withdrawal rates are particularly great for two reasons: first, labour is already taxed at high rates so METRs are already high; and second, the income distributions are particularly narrow, especially those of Denmark and Sweden. As a result, high withdrawal rates over even a small income range would affect a very large number of workers.

Consider making child tax credits more generous to lower the tax burden on families with children

Labour taxes and cash benefits do not vary much with family size and composition. SSCs, which account for the bulk of taxes on labour income, do not differentiate across different family types, and family cash transfers are small and targeted at households in extreme poverty (OECD, forthcoming). Figure 3.8 shows that there is almost no difference between the net take-home pay (income after taxes and transfers) of similar households with and without children, reflecting that the tax and benefit system is rather insensitive to

Figure 3.8. **Net take-home pay ratios between a household with and without children (%) in 2015**

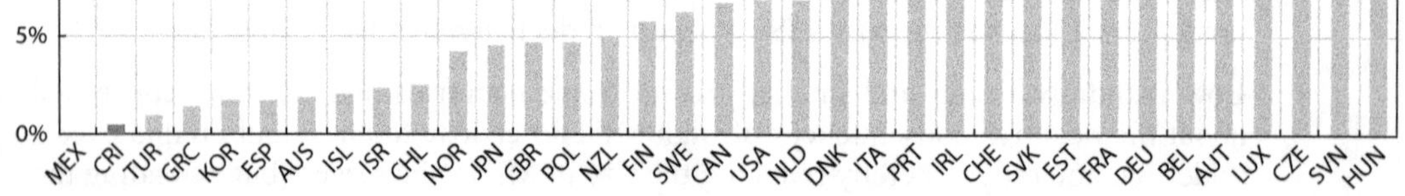

StatLink http://dx.doi.org/10.1787/888933544816

Note: The ratios are calculated as the difference between the net take-home pay (i.e. income after taxes and benefits) between a household with two children and another without any children as a percentage of the net take-home pay of a family without children. Both households are composed of married couples with one spouse earning the average wage in the country and the other spouse earning a third of that amount.

Source: OECD (2016) *Taxing Wages 2016*, and OECD/IDB/CIAT (2016), *Taxing Wages in Latin America and the Caribbean 2016*, OECD Publishing, Paris.

the presence of children in the households (OECD, forthcoming). This contrasts with many OECD countries where the disposable income of households with children is significantly greater than that of similar households without children.

Given that child poverty is high in Costa Rica, making greater use of family tax credits to lower the tax burden on families could be considered. Costa Rica offers a tax credit per child amounting to CRC 16 080 (approximately EUR 27). This level is low compared to similar provisions in OECD countries. If Costa Rica managed to raise additional revenues through the planned tax reforms, it could enhance the generosity of its child tax credit, in particular given the country's poor performance on child poverty indicators (OECD, forthcoming). Increasing child tax credits could also be a way to compensate households for the possible regressive effects of VAT base broadening if the VAT reform is approved.

The "final" withholding of PIT on employment makes it difficult to provide targeted tax support through the PIT system

Generally, the withholding of PIT on employment and other types of income helps to raise tax compliance. Except for Switzerland, PIT levied on employment income is administered in all other OECD countries through a withholding tax system. In Switzerland, PIT is administered at the cantonal level; as cantons are relatively small and individuals may work in a different canton than the canton where they live, PIT withholding becomes more difficult to implement in Switzerland. PIT withholding systems also exist in most major non-OECD countries including Brazil, China, India, and Russia.

Where both withholding taxes and third partly information apply, compliance reaches around 99 percent in advanced countries (IMF, 2015). Imposing the obligation on independent third parties such as employers and financial institutions to withhold an amount of tax from payments of income to taxpayers brings three major advantages. It enhances tax compliance; the timely remittance of amounts withheld by third parties to the revenue body ensures a regular flow of revenue to government and assists budgetary management; it is a more cost efficient way for both taxpayers and the revenue body to transact the payment of taxes (i.e. lower compliance and administrative costs).

Costa Rica implements an imperfect "cumulative" withholding regime for employment income. The cumulative withholding regime aims to ensure that for the majority of employees the total amount of taxes withheld over the course of a fiscal year matches their full (fiscal) year tax liability. To the extent this is achieved, employees are then freed of the obligation to prepare and file an annual tax return, but they are allowed to do so if exceptional circumstances would have resulted in too many taxes having been withheld. Under this approach, employees are required to provide employers with details of relevant entitlements to assist them determine the amount of tax to be deducted from their earnings. In some countries (e.g. Ireland and UK), employees provide this information to the revenue body which in turn advises the employer of a code that determines the amount of tax to be deducted from earnings. Employers withhold tax from income paid, as required, determining amounts to be withheld on a progressive/cumulative basis over the course of the fiscal year. Under the cumulative approach, employees tend to have few entitlements (that reduce tax payable) as this enables greater accuracy in calculating the amount of taxes withheld over the course of a fiscal year vis-à-vis their end-of year tax liabilities. When employees change jobs or have been previously unemployed, the new employer would have to take those changes in income into account in order to again withhold the appropriate amount of taxes such that the total amount of withheld taxes during the year math the full-year tax liability. However, this is not the case in Costa Rica.

Inequities arise as PIT is withheld irrespective of previously earned income. In Costa Rica, PITs are withheld on a monthly basis not taking into account previously earned income during the fiscal year. Taxpayers that face a steady stream of employment income will therefore pay a different amount of tax than employees who earn the same total amount of income over the year, but earn high income in some months and less or no income in other months of the fiscal year. This clearly undermines the fairness of the tax system.

The more common alternative is the "non-cumulative" PIT withholding approach. The "non-cumulative" PIT withholding system operates on a "pay period" basis for each employee. Employers withhold taxes for each pay period having regard to their gross income, taking some but not necessarily all entitlements into account (that may reduce the amount to be withheld) and the rate of withholding to be applied. Where an employee changes jobs, the new employer simply commences the withholding process on the employee's future income without regard to his/her previous employment withholdings. However, as this approach involves a less precise form of withholding, the amount deducted for each employee over the course of a fiscal year represents only an approximation of their full fiscal year's tax liability. In these circumstances, employees are normally required to file annual tax returns to ensure that the correct overall amount of tax is paid (and to obtain a refund of any overpaid tax), taking account of all categories of assessable income and entitlements (e.g. tax deductions and credits).

"Final" withholding of PITs on monthly employment income, as is the case in Costa Rica, makes it difficult to provide targeted tax support through the PIT system. Costa Rica implements two limited tax credits: a monthly tax credit for each dependent child (CRC 1 490) and a monthly tax credit for a spouse in a married couple (CRC 2 230); both tax credits have only a minor impact on the overall tax burden on employment income. Indeed, the fact that taxes on employment income are withheld by the employer on a monthly basis and that these withheld taxes are the final taxes that have to be paid, irrespective of employment income earned in the rest of the year, makes it difficult to provide more targeted support to particular families through the PIT system.

Labour taxes introduce distortions between employees and self-employed and professional workers

In contrast to common practice in OECD countries, the PIT system in Costa Rica taxes employment and personal business income separately. Personal business income has to be declared by the taxpayer on a yearly basis. PIT on employment income, on the other hand, is withheld by the employer on a monthly basis. The tax rates on employment income range from 0% up to monthly income of CRC 793 000 (EUR 1 320), 10% and 15% on monthly employment income exceeding CRC 1 190 000 (EUR 1 980) while personal business income is taxed under a 5-bracket rate schedule with tax rates ranging from 0% to 25% (Table 3.2).

SSCs levied on employment income are significantly higher than SSCs paid by the self-employed. As mentioned before, employee SSCs are levied on employment income at a flat rate of 9.34% in 2015 and employers pay SSCs at a rate of 26.33%. By contrast, the self-employed pay SSCs on their personal business income at rates which are increasing with income and vary between 8.25% and 19.59%. Nevertheless, the total contribution rate is the same for all self-employed workers, irrespective of their income, because, unlike any OECD country, the central government contributes for self-employed workers' health, maternity and first-tier pension (with the government contribution rate decreasing with income). Another major difference between the tax treatment of employees and self-employed workers is that, contrary to employees who are required to pay a minimum amount of SSCs if their earnings are below a certain threshold, independent workers earning below that minimum contribution base are exempt from contributions.

Table 3.2. **Personal income tax rates: employment income (Panel A) and business income (Panel B), 2016**

A. Employment income *Monthly PIT rate schedule*		B. Business income *Annual PIT rate schedule*	
up to 792 000	exempt	up to 3 517 000	exempt
792 001 – 1 188 000	10	3 517 001 – 5 251 000	10
over 1 188 000	15	5 251 001 – 8 760 000	15
		8 760 001 – 17 556 000	20
		over 17 556 000	25

Source: IBFD Database.

Differences in the tax treatment between employees and self-employed workers create significant incentives to work as independent workers as well as tax avoidance opportunities. The much lower SSC burden on self-employed workers as well as the absence of a minimum level of contributions provides incentives for formal workers to work as independent workers. In addition, in order to lower their overall tax burden on labour income, formal workers may have an incentive to work part-time as employees and the rest of the time as self-employed workers. This allows workers to benefit from the exempt amount of income under both tax rate schedules and to spread their total income into two separate taxable sources which implies that less income will be taxed at top PIT rates. This tax treatment violates the horizontal equity tax principle, as taxpayers earning the same amount of income but receiving it through different sources are taxed differently. It also violates vertical equity as higher income earners do not necessarily pay higher taxes than lower income workers. The different tax withholding approaches and the lower SSCs for self-employed workers have also provided incentives for employers to hire "dependent workers" in the form of self-employed labour. A better alignment between the SSCs paid by self-employed workers and employees could help address this issue.

Costa Rica also suffers from widespread tax avoidance in liberal professions

Tax avoidance is widespread among liberal professions. Income earned by professionals such as lawyers, architects, doctors, dentists and accountants through the rendering of independent professional services, is taxed in the same manner as personal business income. For professionals who do not maintain accounting records or do not issue receipts, they pay taxes over a presumed income. The presumption is either 250 or 335 times the basis salary depending on the profession. However, tax avoidance by those professions was reported as a critical issue. A report found that in 2015, about 55% of the physical and legal persons rendering profitable professional service activities declared zero income tax (Figure 3.9). On average, this share remained relatively constant over the 2011-15 period at an average of 56% (report *Contraloria General de la Republica*). The share of professionals who reported zero income tax is particularly high in accounting and auditing and information and technology (IT) services (Figure 3.9). The report also found that a total of 53 005 taxpayers (86% of the total), accounted for about 48% of assets and 30% of gross earnings of the total group; while accounting for only 9% of total taxes paid (Table 3.3).

Figure 3.9. **Share of taxpayers declaring zero income tax in different liberal professions in 2015**

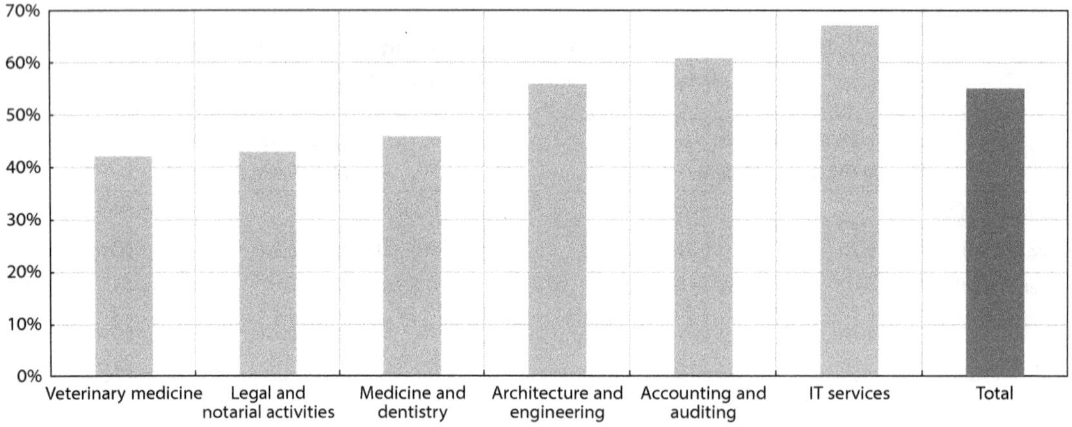

StatLink http://dx.doi.org/10.1787/888933544835

Source: CGR (2016).

Table 3.3. **Income tax declared by liberal professionals in 2015**

Income tax declared (in CRC)	Number of taxpayers	% of taxpayers	% of taxes paid	% of gross earnings	% of assets
Equal to zero	33 527	54.8%	0.0%	9.6%	21.9%
[1 – 500 001]	19 478	31.8%	9.1%	20.2%	26.5%
[500 – 1 000 001]	3 042	5.0%	7.1%	7.9%	7.0%
[1 000 001 – 1 500 001]	1 430	2.3%	5.8%	5.2%	5.0%
[1 500 001 – 2 000 001]	850	1.4%	4.8%	4.3%	3.5%
[2 000 001 – 2 500 001]	599	1.0%	4.4%	3.5%	2.7%
[2 500 001 – 3 000 001]	323	0.5%	2.9%	2.3%	1.8%
[3 000 001 – 10 000 001]	1 489	2.4%	25.9%	17.1%	13.2%
Over 10 000 001	471	0.8%	39.8%	29.8%	18.4%
Total	61 209	100%	100%	100%	100%

Source: CGR (2016).

Liberal professions can easily underreport their income or overstate deductible expenses. Many professionals do not receive payments for their services via debit or credit cards and do not issue receipts for payments in cash, which allows them to underreport their income. Liberal professions can also easily over-report deductible expenses or claim expenses that should not be claimed (e.g. inclusion of personal expenses or partners' expenses such as luxury vehicles, high-value property, the construction and/or interest payments on housing, land acquisition, school payments for children).

Widespread tax evasion among liberal professions undermines the integrity of the tax system. Tax evasion by liberal professions significantly erodes tax revenues. It also undermines the integrity and the fairness of the tax system and ultimately negatively affects tax morale. Finally, this form of evasion is likely to reduce the overall progressivity of the tax system as professionals tend to earn high incomes.

Further efforts are needed to reduce tax avoidance among liberal professions. Establishing rules requiring all professionals to maintain accounting records and issue receipts would increase tax compliance. In addition, mandatory electronic invoicing should be speeded up to address the underreporting of income. This process has been delayed several times; the government is now developing a system to use digital invoices which is expected to be launched in June 2017. A stricter definition of deductible expenses should also be considered. For instance, deductions from taxable income of expenses paid in cash above a low minimum threshold could be disallowed. The tax administration should also be granted more authority to control deductible expenses. In theory, the tax administration may disallow the deduction of payments deemed excessive but the Administrative Court ruled in Decision 122-07 that the tax administration cannot disallow expenses only through the application of the economic reality principle and that all documentation (usually invoices and accounting records) provided by the taxpayer as proof must be taken into consideration. Finally, more targeted audits focusing on riskier professions are needed to fight tax avoidance and evasion by professionals.

The planned VAT reform could indirectly strengthen PIT compliance among liberal professions. The reform plans to apply VAT broadly to services (with a few remaining exceptions). Thus, businesses would have to be registered to be able to deduct input VAT on their business to business (B2B) transactions. Costa Rica could also consider providing a PIT credit for the VAT paid on certain services.

PIT does not contribute to income redistribution

The top PIT rate for employees is low in comparison with OECD and LAC countries. The current top PIT rate of 15% on income exceeding CRC 1 181 000 is much lower than the average top PIT rate in OECD countries which reached 43.6% in 2015 (Figure 3.10). The only country in the OECD that has a similar statutory top PIT rate is the Czech Republic, which is an uncommon case as Czech Republic has a flat PIT rate and the taxable base is labour costs as opposed to gross earnings (meaning that employee and employer SSCs are taxable). Costa Rica's top PIT rate is also low compared to LAC countries (Figure 3.11). Costa Rica's relatively low top statutory PIT rate may be partly explained by the fact that it starts being levied at relatively low income levels (Figure 3.12).

The 2017 tax reform proposal includes an increase in the top PIT rate with the inclusion of two additional tax brackets and rates. Employment income would become subject to two additional tax brackets: incomes exceeding CRC 2 225 000 and income above CRC 4 450 000 would respectively be taxed at the rates of 20% and 25%. This would increase PIT progressivity and bring Costa Rica closer to top PIT rates in OECD and other LAC countries. This would also be in line with recent trends of top PIT rate increases in OECD countries (OECD, 2016).

Figure 3.10. **Top statutory PIT rates in Costa Rica and OECD countries in 2015**

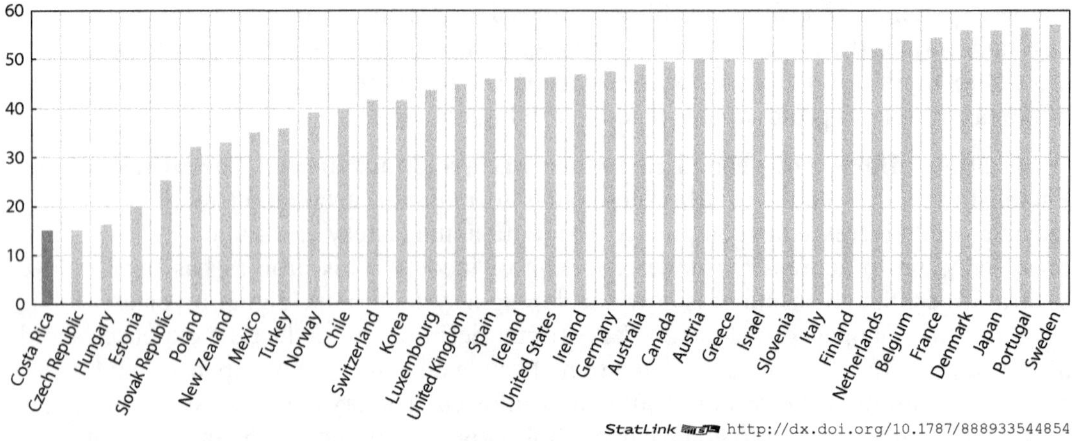

StatLink http://dx.doi.org/10.1787/888933544854

Note: Information on data for Israel: http://dx.doi.org/10.1787/888932315602.

Source: OECD Tax Database.

Figure 3.11. **Top statutory PIT rates in LAC countries in 2016**

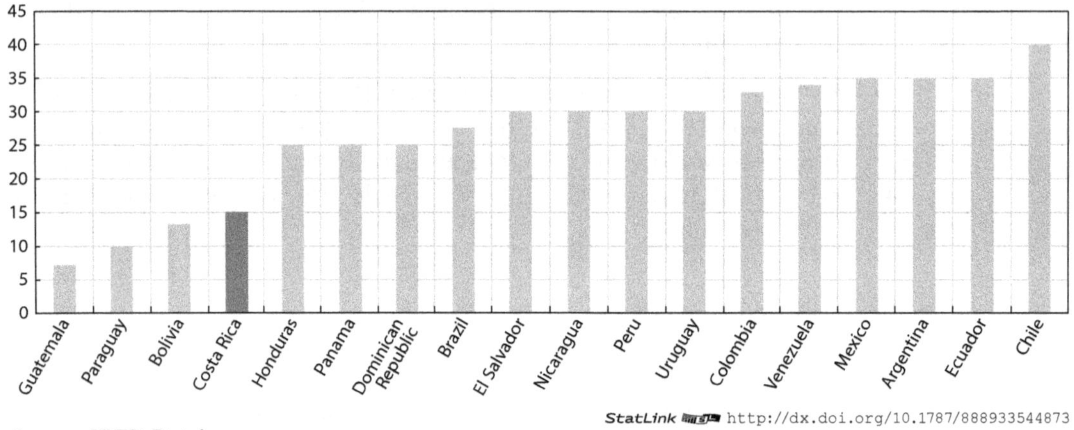

StatLink http://dx.doi.org/10.1787/888933544873

Source: IBFD Database.

Figure 3.12. **Top statutory PIT rates and income levels levied in LAC countries**

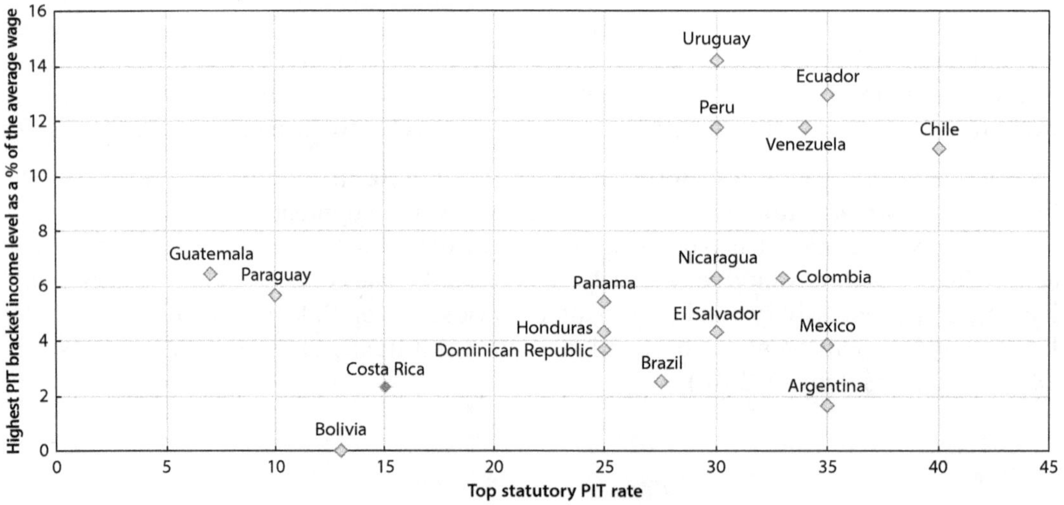

StatLink http://dx.doi.org/10.1787/888933544892

Source: Based on Barreix et al. (2017).

Effective PIT rates show that PIT is progressive in Costa Rica but that effective PIT burdens are very low, including for high-income earners. Table 3.4 shows what proportion of gross income has been effectively paid as income tax across income deciles. In Costa Rica, PIT payments as a share of income increase with income, which means that PIT is effectively progressive. However, average PIT rates are very low, including for taxpayers in the top income decile. Indeed, average PIT rates in the top income decile amount to about 4.5%, far below the statutory tax rate of 15%. This rate is also low in comparison to effective PIT rates on top income earners in many other LAC countries. Additional PIT brackets and rates would contribute to further increasing progressivity and raising the tax burden on high-income earners but those measures would also have to be accompanied by base broadening measures and stricter tax enforcement.

Table 3.4. **Personal income tax: observed average rates by income decile**

Deciles	I	II	III	IV	V	VI	VII	VIII	IX	X	Average
Argentina	2.6	3.1	3.9	6	7.7	8.6	10.1	11.9	14.3	20.5	**8.9**
Bolivia	0	0	0.6	2.6	4.1	5.4	6.7	7.7	8.8	11.3	**4.7**
Chile	0	0	0	0	0	0.1	0.1	0.3	0.8	10.4	**1.2**
Costa Rica	0	0	0.1	0.1	0.1	0.3	0.4	1.2	1.9	4.5	**0.9**
Honduras	0	0	0	0	0	0	0	0	0	5.8	**0.6**
Ecuador	0	0	0	0	0	0	0	0.3	0.9	2.6	**0.4**
Mexico	-0.2	0	0.3	0.9	1.1	1.6	2.8	3.3	5.8	6.8	**2.2**
Paraguay	0	0	0	0	0	0	0	0	0	0.03	**0**
Peru	0.2	0.3	0.4	0.4	0.3	0.3	0.5	0.7	2.8	13.2	**1.9**
Dominican Republic	0	0	0	0	0	0	0	0	0.9	12.6	**1.4**
Uruguay	0	0	0	0	0	0.1	1.5	4.5	8.3	14	**2.8**
Average	**0.2**	**0.3**	**0.5**	**0.9**	**1.2**	**1.5**	**2**	**2.7**	**4**	**9.2**	**2.3**

Note: The rates derive from the ratio between the tax or resulting benefit, in the case of refunds, in the tax year and the gross income of each income decile according to the returns received by the tax administrations. The rates indicate what proportion of gross income has been effectively paid as income tax.

Source: Barreix et al. (2017).

Despite being progressive, the very limited revenues from PIT constrain the income tax's redistributive effect. In OECD countries, even if transfers typically play a much greater role in narrowing income gaps, taxes – in particular PIT – have an important effect on income redistribution. On average, three quarters of the reduction in inequality between market and disposable incomes are due to transfers while taxes account for the remaining quarter of income redistribution (Figure 3.13). In Costa Rica, however, PIT does not contribute to reducing income inequality. Even if the PIT is designed to be progressive, in practice it raises far too little revenue to have an effect on the distribution of income. Limited revenues from PIT is one of the factors accounting for the very small difference between Gini coefficients before and after taxes and transfers in Costa Rica compared to other countries (Figure 3.13).

Figure 3.13. **Reduction in income inequality due to direct taxes and cash benefits in 2013**

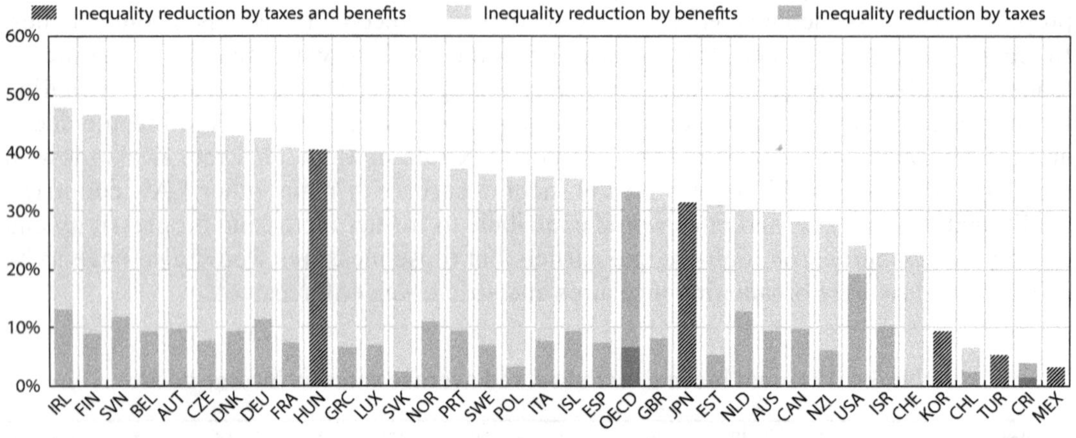

StatLink http://dx.doi.org/10.1787/888933544911

Notes: Data refers to 2009 for Japan; 2011 for Canada; 2013 for Chile; 2015 for Costa Rica. OECD refers to the simple (unweighted) average of the OECD countries.

Source: OECD (forthcoming), OECD Reviews of Labour Market and Social Policies: Costa Rica, based on OECD Income Distribution Database, http://oe.cd/idd.

The lack of integration between the PIT and SSC systems limits the efficiency and redistributive potential of labour taxes

There is a lack of integration between the PIT and SSC systems in Costa Rica. The Costa Rican social security system is divided into different institutions including the *Caja Costarricense de Seguridad Social* (CCSS), the *Fondo de Desarrollo Social y Asignaciones Familiares* (FODESAF), IMAS and INA. The CCSS is by far the largest one and constitutes a separate distribution mechanism which needs to balance its own budget. This is particularly challenging as certain welfare provisions, such as health care, are "universally" available also to households which did not pay matching social security contributions. This is the case, for instance, for workers in the informal sector. In order to prevent extreme poverty among the elderly, workers in the informal economy are also entitled to an, albeit very low, minimum pension. In addition, the CCSS is entitled to raise SSC rates without the Parliament's approval, which creates uncertainty for workers and employers.

The lack of integration between the PIT and SSC system lies at the heart of the labour market challenges which Costa Rica is facing. Because they have to finance their own expenditure, social security funds including the CCSS end up levying very high tax rates, without taking into consideration the economic impact of SSCs on work incentives and on the cost of employment. It results also in large incentives for workers and their employers to continue working in the informal economy.

In addition to funding social security programmes, Costa Rican SSCs are used to fund programmes other than social security programmes. This raises the tax wedge on labour income even further, which in turn deters the creation and formalisation of employment, and reduces the progressivity of the tax system (see above). The government should avoid using SSCs to fund public banks and antipoverty programmes and should rely, for those purposes, on other more progressive taxes such as PIT. However, this shift in financing would require a greater integration across the different institutions in the social security system as well as between the PIT and the SSC systems.

A better integration between the PIT and SSC systems could be achieved in different ways. Countries' experiences differ in that regard. Of the 32 OECD countries with SSC regimes, 13 have integrated their collection with tax administration operations while the rest administer their collection through separate social security bodies (although integration has also been considered as a possibility in the future or is being studied in Czech Republic, Greece, Portugal and Slovak Republic). In those countries where separate arrangements exist for tax and SSC collection, the overlapping nature of the revenue collection responsibilities of the different bodies and their client base present opportunities for co-operation and mutual assistance. This occurs in various ways, e.g. through the use of common audit programmes, information exchange between agencies, assistance with enforced collection of unpaid SSCs and collaboration to streamline information exchange procedures (OECD, 2015). In general, this highlights the importance of digitisation and exchange of information. In that sense, Costa Rica should move towards adopting a system where fiscal and SSC information can be linked together.

The tax policy recommendations that can be drawn from this analysis are as follows:

Recommendations

- Lower the PIT threshold under which no PIT has to be paid.
- Make employee SSCs deductible for personal income tax purposes.
- Levy all SSCs as a share of actual income.
- Consider lowering the tax burden on low-income workers by lowering SSCs or introducing an earned income tax credit.
- Consider funding some social benefits, in particular non-contributory programmes such as FODESAF and IMAS, through general taxes.
- Possibly enhance the generosity of family tax credits to lower the tax burden on families with children.
- Tax employment and personal business income under the same PIT rate schedule.
- Introduce additional PIT brackets and, in particular, raise the top PIT rate over time.
- Move from a monthly assessment basis towards an annual assessment of PITs levied on employment income and allow taxpayers who earn employment income to file a tax return at the end of the year.
- Increase efforts to address tax evasion by liberal professions.
- Better integrate the PIT and SSC system, in particular through enhanced exchange of information.

Note

1. Table III.1 in the OECD Tax Database provides more information on the deductibility of employee SSCs from the personal income tax base: see www.oecd.org/ctp/tax-policy/Table%20III.1-Mar-2015.xlsx.

References

Andrews, D., A. Caldera Sánchez and Å. Johansson (2011), "Towards a Better Understanding of the Informal Economy", *OECD Economics Department Working Papers*, No. 873, OECD Publishing, Paris, http://dx.doi.org/10.1787/5kgb1mf88x28-en.

Barreix A., J.C. Benitez and M. Pecho (2017), "Revisiting personal income tax", *OECD Development Centre Working Papers*, OECD Publishing, Paris, http://dx.doi.org/10.1787/16d42b4a-en.

Brys, B., S. Perret, A. Thomas and P. O'Reilly (2016), "Tax design for inclusive economic growth", *OECD Taxation Working Papers*, No. 26, OECD Publishing, Paris, http://dx.doi.org/10.1787/5jlv74ggk0g7-en.

CGR (2016), *Informe de Auditoría de Carácter Especial sobre el Impuesto a las utilidades de las Personas Físicas y Jurídicas, con Actividad Económica Lucrativa, que Prestan Servicios Profesionales*, [Special audit report on the tax on the profits of individuals and legal entities, with a lucrative economic activity, providing professional services], INFORME No. DFOE-SAF-IF-14-2016.

IMF (2015), "Current challenges in revenue mobilization: improving tax compliance", *Policy Papers*, IMF Staff Report.

Lehmann, H. and A. Muravyev (2012), "Labour market institutions and informality in transition and Latin American countries", *IZA Discussion Papers*, No. 7035, Bonn.

OECD (Forthcoming – 2017), *OECD Reviews of Labour Market and Social Policies: Costa Rica,* OECD Publishing, Paris.

OECD (2016), *Taxing Wages 2016*, OECD Publishing, Paris, http://dx.doi.org/10.1787/tax_wages-2016-en.

OECD (2015), *Tax Administration 2015: Comparative Information on OECD and other Advanced and Emerging Economies*, OECD Publishing, Paris, http://dx.doi.org/10.1787/tax_admin-2015-en.

OECD/IDB/CIAT (2016), *Taxing Wages in Latin America and the Caribbean 2016*, OECD Publishing, Paris, http://dx.doi.org/10.1787/9789264262607-en.

Perry, G., W. Maloney, O. Arias, P. Fajnzylber, A. Mason and J. Saavedra (2007), "Informality: exit and exclusion", *The World Bank Latin American and Caribbean Studies*, The World Bank, Washington, DC.

Torres, C., K. Mellbye and B. Brys (2012), "Trends in personal income tax and employee social security contribution schedules", *OECD Taxation Working Papers*, No. 12, OECD Publishing, Paris, http://dx.doi.org/10.1787/5k95qw9633vf-en.

Chapter 4

Putting in place a modern VAT system in Costa Rica

This chapter discusses the sales tax in Costa Rica, which has a narrow tax base and does not apply to services in general. The impact on domestic and international trade of the sales tax is discussed. The chapter also focuses on the regressivity of the sales tax at the top of the income distribution as a result of sales tax exemptions which primarily benefit the wealthy. Costa Rica is planning to introduce a well-designed and broad-based valued added tax (VAT) system, covering both goods and services, to be able to generate additional revenues and remove existing sales tax distortions. Costa Rica's plans to mitigate the distributional effects of a broad-based VAT through well-targeted transfers are also discussed.

The statistical data for Israel are supplied by and under the responsibility of the relevant Israeli authorities. The use of such data by the OECD is without prejudice to the status of the Golan Heights, East Jerusalem and Israeli settlements in the West Bank under the terms of international law.

Revenues from the sales tax are below revenues from typical VAT systems in comparable countries

Revenues from the sales tax are comparatively low. In Costa Rica, revenues from the general sales tax amounted to about 4.7% of GDP and 21.1% of total tax revenues in 2014. This is low compared to average VAT revenues in OECD countries and other Latin American and Caribbean (LAC) countries. In OECD countries, VAT revenues accounted on average for 6.6% of GDP and 19.5% of total tax revenues in 2013 while VAT revenues accounted for around 6.3 % of GDP and 29.8% of total tax revenues on average in Latin American countries in 2014 (Figure 4.1). As discussed below, the main factor which explains Costa Rica's comparatively low sales tax revenues is the tax's very narrow base.

Figure 4.1. **VAT revenues as a share of GDP in LAC countries and OECD average in 2014**

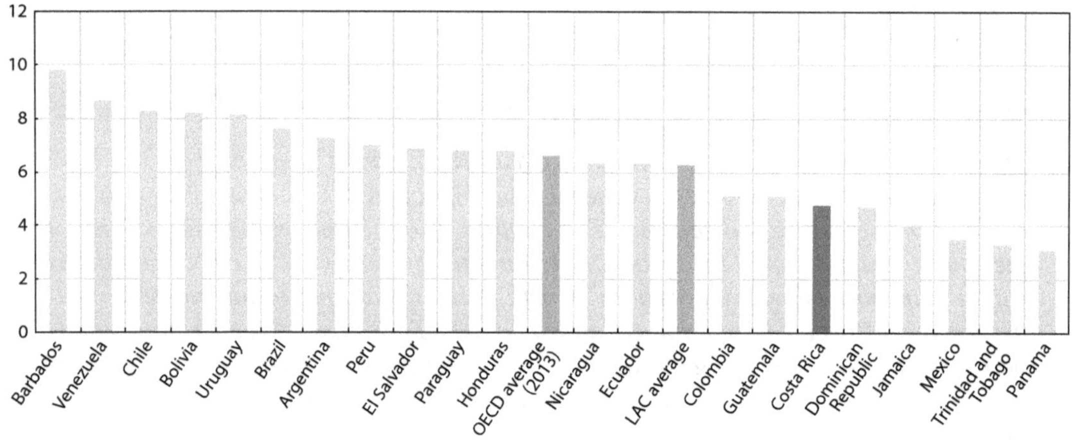

StatLink http://dx.doi.org/10.1787/888933544930

Source: OECD Revenue Statistics.

The reform which is currently being discussed is expected to generate most of the revenue increase from changes in the VAT system. The VAT reform is expected to generate additional revenues amounting to 1% of GDP, while the income tax reform is expected to generate additional revenues of about 0.6% of GDP. The main changes proposed as part of the VAT reform include a significant broadening of the tax base to cover all services. This reform would help bring Costa Rica's VAT revenues closer to levels in comparable countries but will be insufficient to address the country's fiscal sustainability challenges (see Chapter 1).

Raising additional revenues through VAT could be less detrimental to economic growth than raising revenues through alternative and more growth-distorting taxes. The *OECD's Tax and Economic Growth* report from 2010, which assessed four major categories of taxes in terms of their negative impact on long-run GDP per capita, ranked consumption taxes as the second least damaging to economic growth after recurrent taxes on immovable property and before other property taxes and personal and corporate income taxes (OECD, 2010). VAT is therefore generally considered as a comparatively efficient tax to raise revenues, in particular for a country with a relatively low standard VAT rate such as Costa Rica. In addition, as discussed further in the chapter, a well-designed VAT system can provide incentives for businesses to enter the formal sector and thereby contribute to reducing informality (see below).

Costa Rica's sales tax has a very narrow base and does not apply to services in general

Costa Rica's general sales tax has a very narrow base. The current general sales tax is levied on all goods except for the goods which are explicitly exempted by the law. Exempt goods include the goods in the basic consumption basket (*canasta básica*) which consists of more than 250 goods; essential goods for education; medicines; agricultural inputs; a number of cultural goods; kerosene; and the monthly consumption of electric energy when it does not exceed 250 kW/h. For services, on the other hand, the sales tax is generally not levied, except for services that are explicitly included in the law. Taxable services include restaurants and hotels, internet access, insurance services, telecommunication services, cinema tickets, and the maintenance and repair of cars as well as services rendered by repair shops for all types of merchandise. All the services that are not expressly mentioned in the law are not subject to the sales tax. Examples of exempt services include medical care, education, professional services and construction services. Because it generally exempts services, the current general sales tax in Costa Rica does not have the basic features of a modern VAT system.

The narrow sales tax base causes a significant loss in potential revenues. According to the latest tax expenditure report, the sales tax expenditures for exempt goods amounted to 1.44% of GDP while tax expenditures for exempt services amounted to 1.19% of GDP in 2015. In comparison, total tax expenditures under the income tax were estimated at around 1.84% of GDP. It is important to note that the current sales tax was inherited from the early 1980s and that the share of services in total consumption has significantly increased since then. Thus, exempting a large number of services has represented an increasingly significant revenue loss for Costa Rica.

Costa Rica's narrow sales tax base results in a low VAT revenue ratio. The VAT revenue ratio (VRR) is the ratio between the revenue actually collected from VAT (or sales tax in Costa Rica's case) and the revenue that would be raised if the standard VAT rate (or sales tax rate) were applied uniformly to all final consumption and perfectly administered and enforced. It is therefore an indicator of both the broadness of the VAT base and the effectiveness of the tax administration in enforcing the VAT. As shown in Figure 4.2, Costa Rica's VAT revenue ratio is 0.46, which is low in comparison to both LAC and OECD averages. It means that 54% of total consumption in Costa Rica effectively escapes taxation

Figure 4.2. **VAT revenue ratios in LAC countries and OECD average in 2014**

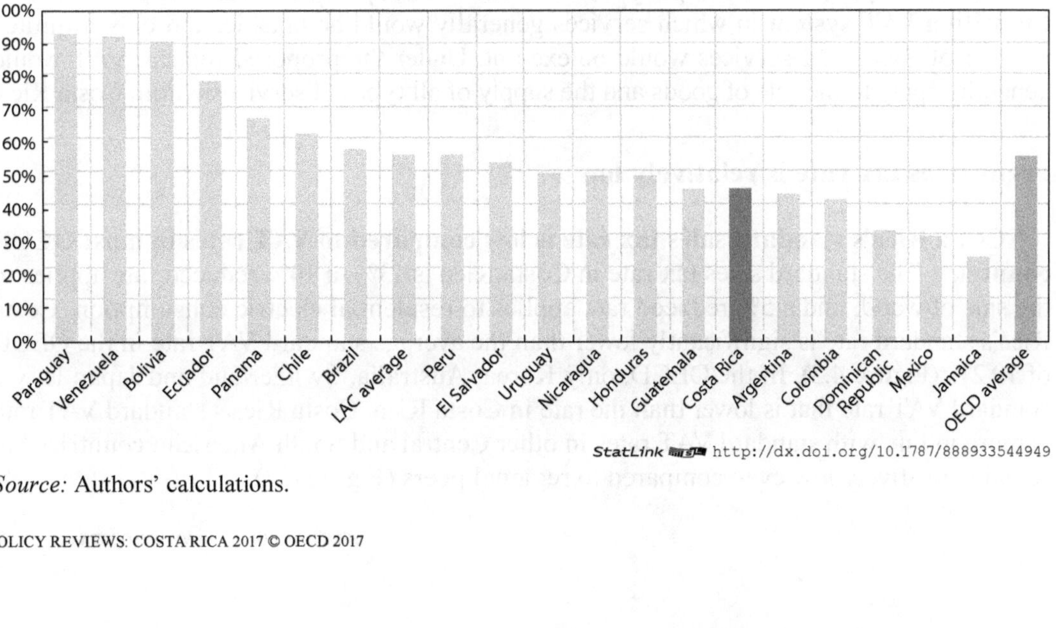

StatLink http://dx.doi.org/10.1787/888933544949

Source: Authors' calculations.

at the standard VAT rate. Costa Rica's low VRR level reflects to a large extent the narrowness of Costa Rica's VAT base, in combination with the existence of tax evasion (see below).

In addition, not taxing services greatly reduces the sales tax's neutrality. For services that are not taxed, sales tax on inputs cannot be recovered, which means that the sales tax constitutes a direct cost for businesses providing tax-exempt services in contrast to domestic producers of taxable services which can deduct the sales tax paid on their inputs. Internationally, Costa Rican services destined to be consumed outside of Costa Rica are exempt from the sales tax, without the right to deduct the sales tax incurred on associated inputs, which in turn makes them less competitive compared to service providers in other countries that can deduct input VAT. Indeed, the prices of Costa Rican services consumed outside of Costa Rica include the costs of the goods that were used to produce those services but the sales tax paid on those goods cannot be recovered. The unrecoverable sales tax will typically be embedded in the sales price, thereby putting Costa Rican service companies at a competitive disadvantage. This goes against the fundamental neutrality principles of a VAT according to which the VAT burden should not lie on businesses but on final consumers and according to which foreign businesses should not be disadvantaged or advantaged compared to domestic businesses.

Taxing goods but not services also poses challenges in relation to sales whose price includes a goods and services component. The general sales tax rules in Costa Rica imply that, in principle, the sales price has to be split into a price for the taxable goods and a component for the tax-exempt services that are sold together with the goods. This generates an incentive to over-price the untaxed services and under-price the taxed goods in order to minimise the tax that has to be paid on the sale price; this possibility to minimise the sales tax would then also induce businesses to sell combined goods and services. In order to prevent those tax base erosion practices from happening, Costa Rica levies the sales tax on the share of the price that relates to the services that are offered together with the goods, even if those services are tax-exempt if they would be sold separately. Only the value of services that are provided by third parties and are invoiced and registered separately is tax-exempt. As a result, Costa Rican businesses that offer combined goods and services (i.e. the sales tax will be levied on the full price) face a competitive disadvantage to businesses that offer the services separately (as no tax might be due on those services). The current sales tax might therefore distort commercial decisions of businesses on how to organise their activities. In practice, however, many of the services that are typically sold together with goods, such as repair and maintenance, have been explicitly included as taxable services in the law.

The main purpose of the proposed reform is to replace the current general sales tax with a VAT system in which services generally would be taxable, and only a limited number of goods and services would be exempt. Under the proposed reform, VAT would generally apply to the sale of goods and the supply of all types of services within Costa Rica.

The current sales tax rate is relatively low

Costa Rica's standard sales tax rate is low compared to VAT rates in most OECD countries. The standard sales tax rate in Costa Rica is 13%; a 10% reduced rate applies to the sale of wood, and a 5% reduced rate applies to residential electric consumption. Costa Rica's standard rate is significantly lower than the average standard VAT rate in the OECD of 19.2% (Figure 4.3). In the OECD, only Korea, Australia, Switzerland and Japan levy a standard VAT rate that is lower than the rate in Costa Rica. Costa Rica's standard VAT rate is more in line with standard VAT rates in other Central and South American countries but remains relatively low even compared to regional peers (Figure 4.4).

Figure 4.3. **Standard VAT rates in OECD countries and Costa Rica in 2016**

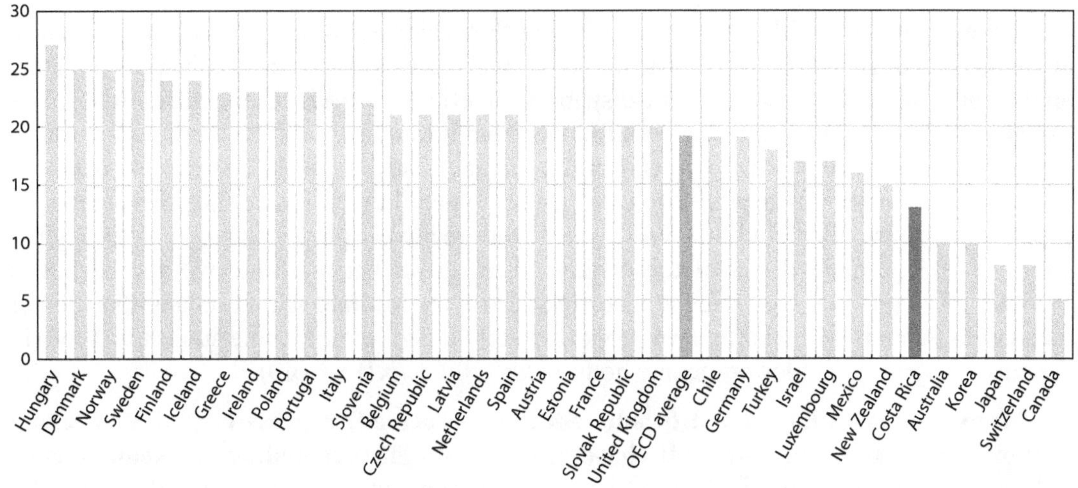

StatLink http://dx.doi.org/10.1787/888933544968

Notes: 1. The overall VAT rate in Canada is about 15% on average when the HST or provincial sales taxes are taken into account.

2. Information on data for Israel: http://dx.doi.org/10.1787/888932315602.

Source: OECD Tax Database.

Figure 4.4. **Standard VAT rates in Central and South American countries in 2016**

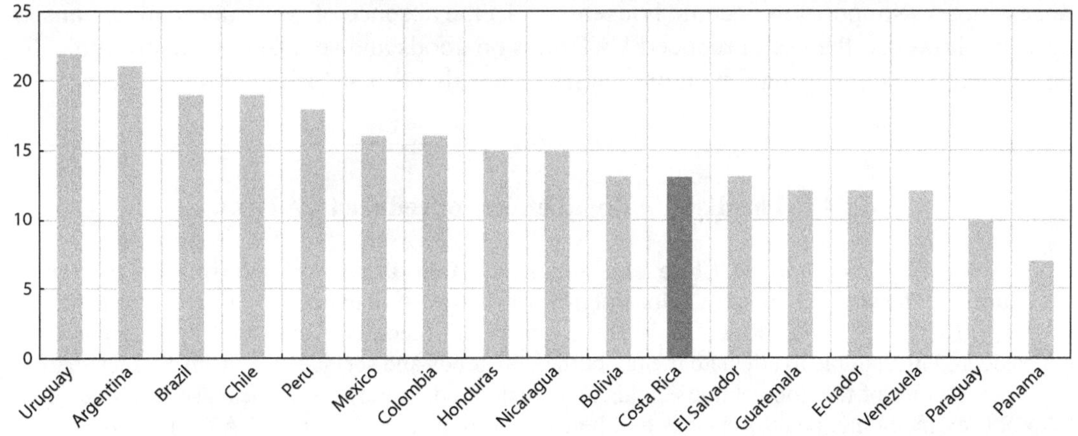

StatLink http://dx.doi.org/10.1787/888933544987

Source: KPMG.

With the reform, the standard VAT rate would be maintained and a new reduced VAT rate would be introduced. The initial reform proposal was to raise the standard rate to 15% and have a reduced tax rate of 5%, which would increase gradually, on the inputs of some of the goods and services that continue to be exempt, including equipment and machinery used for the production of goods in the basic consumption basket, raw materials used for the production of medicine, services used in the production of agricultural or agro-industrial products and plane tickets for domestic or international flights initiated in Costa Rica. The latest reform bill proposes maintaining the standard VAT rate at 13% and having a reduced VAT rate of 4%. According to the latest reform bill, the reduced rate would also apply to private education services and health services.

The current general sales tax is also regressive

A major concern with VAT systems is that they are perceived as regressive, although evidence has been mixed. VAT is generally perceived as a tax bearing disproportionately on the poor. However, findings on the distributional effects of VAT differ across studies. The conclusion that VAT is a regressive tax follows from the analysis of VAT burdens measured as a percentage of current income across the income distribution. In contrast, studies that present VAT burdens as a proportion of current expenditure across either the income or expenditure distribution find that VAT systems are relatively proportional, or even slightly progressive. The main driver of the difference in results between the two approaches is savings behaviour. Savings rates tend to increase with income, which means that higher income households will tend to have proportionately less of their income subject to VAT (in the current period) than lower income households (OECD/KIPF, 2014).

Many countries have tried to address the (perceived) regressivity of VAT using exemptions or reduced rates but those are rarely well-targeted. VAT exemptions or reduced rates have been widely used as a way to support the poor. Examples typically include VAT exemptions or reduced rates on food and other basic necessities. Those exemptions or reduced rates are generally not well targeted, however. Evidence shows that, at least in OECD countries, while they typically provide greater support to the poor than to the rich as a proportion of household income or expenditure, in absolute value, rich households benefit at best equally but often much more than poor households from reduced VAT rates. This is not surprising as better off households consume more, and often more expensive, products than poorer households. Thus, the general recommendation for OECD countries has been to use direct cash transfers, as opposed to reduced VAT rates on basic necessities, to support low-income households. In the absence of well-functioning transfer systems, however, the use of reduced VAT rates on goods and services which are typically consumed by the poor might be more justified; see also Box 4.1 (OECD/KIPF, 2014).

Box 4.1. **The distributional effects of reduced VAT rates**

With the exceptions of Chile and Japan, all OECD countries have one or more reduced VAT rates to support various policy objectives. A major reason for the introduction of a differentiated rate structure is the promotion of equity. Countries have generally considered it desirable to alleviate the tax burden on goods and services that form a larger share of expenditure of the poorest households (e.g. basic food, water). Countries also often decide to not tax medicine, health services and housing at high rates. Reduced VAT rates have also been used to stimulate the consumption of "merit" goods (e.g. cultural products and education) and other non-distributional objectives such as promoting locally supplied labour-intensive activities (e.g. tourism) and correcting externalities (e.g. energy-saving appliances).

In general, VAT exemptions, zero-rates and reduced rates are not a well-targeted tool to support low-income households. Reduced rates that are implemented in countries for the distinct purpose of supporting the poor (i.e. to address distributional goals) typically do have the desired progressive effect. For example, reduced rates for basic food provide in general greater support to the poor than the rich as a proportion of household income or expenditure. However, despite this progressive effect, these reduced VAT rates are a very poor tool for targeting support to poor households. At best, rich households receive roughly as much benefit – in absolute value – from a reduced rate as do poor households. At worst, rich households benefit vastly more than poor households. This result is unsurprising as better off households can be expected to consume more, and often more expensive, products than poorer

Box 4.1. **The distributional effects of reduced VAT rates** *(continued)*

households. Thus, while poorer households may benefit from reduced VAT rates on "necessities" the wealthier gain even more (OECD/KIPF, 2014).

Cash transfer programmes that cover the entire population, if well-functioning, are a more effective tool to compensate poor households for the VAT they have paid. If poor households can be compensated directly through a cash transfer programme, it is more efficient and fair to tax all goods and services at the standard VAT rate and compensate the poor directly through cash transfers (and/ or reductions in personal income taxes, etc.), especially if the standard VAT rate is not particularly high. It should immediately be noted, however, that compensating all (and only the) losers of a reform through a transfer programme might in practice be very difficult to achieve.

Distributional arguments in favour of VAT rate differentiation may be more persuasive where countries do not have the administrative capacity to provide more direct transfers to poorer households. In the absence of well-functioning cash transfer programmes that can reach the poor, levying a low or even a zero rate VAT on the goods that are typically consumed by poorer households might be considered, at least in the short run.

With regard to preferential VAT provisions for social, cultural and other non-distributional goals, richer households benefit considerably more from VAT exemptions and reduced rates. Those tax provisions often provide so large a benefit to rich households that the reduced VAT rate actually has a regressive effect – benefiting the rich more both in aggregate terms and as a proportion of expenditure. For example, reduced rates on hotel accommodation and restaurant food benefit the rich vastly more than the poor, both in aggregate and proportional terms, in all OECD countries in which they are applied. Similar results, but of less absolute magnitude, are found for reduced rates on books, cinema, theatre and concerts.

Finally, VAT rate differentiation might not be the best policy instrument to correct negative externalities. VAT rate differentiation may improve efficiency if it means that the private marginal costs of an activity are brought closer to the marginal costs for society. However, VAT is a blunt instrument for correcting environmental externalities, as it may be hard to target the actual source of pollution. For example, reduced rates on energy-saving appliances may boost demand or them and therefore stimulate the consumption of these goods. The reduced VAT rate may give incentives to shift from more to less energy-consuming items (consumers might replace their old refrigerator with a new one, for instance). However, this may also lead to an increase in the purchase of energy-intensive products (e.g. consumers may replace their old refrigerator with a new refrigerator and a freezer). (Copenhagen Economics 2007, Study on Reduced VAT Applied to Goods and Services in Member States in the EU).

Source: OECD/KIPF (2014).

In Costa Rica, the sales tax burden is proportional for low and middle-income households and slightly regressive for the richest households. Figure 4.5 shows the distribution of the sales tax burden as a share of consumption per income decile. It suggests that the tax burden is roughly proportional until the seventh income decile, but becomes regressive after the eighth decile. For instance, while sales tax payments amount to 5.9% of consumption on average for the 10 percent lowest income earners, they account for 4.6% of consumption on average for the top 10 percent income earners. This suggests that richer households spend a greater proportion of their total expenditure on items that are not taxed.

Figure 4.5. **Distribution of the sales tax burden as a share of consumption expenditure per income decile**

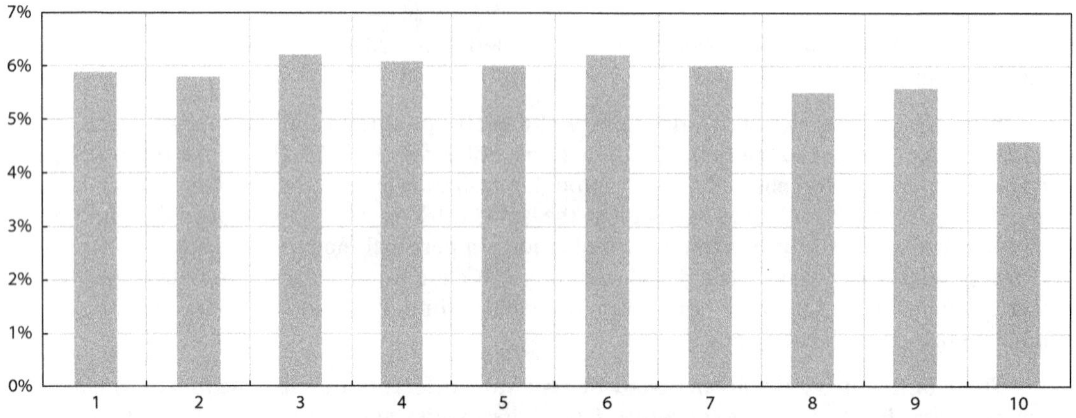

StatLink http://dx.doi.org/10.1787/888933545006

Source: Ministerio de Hacienda (2016).

The regressivity of VAT at the top of the income distribution reflects the fact that sales tax exemptions primarily benefit richer people. As in many other countries, VAT or sales tax exemptions are regressive. Figure 4.6 shows that the bottom 30% benefit from only 17% of the exemptions while the 30% richest receive three times more (51%). Exempting services has negative distributional effects as they represent a higher share of consumption for higher income households. Services represent a greater share of total consumption for richer than poorer households. Figure 4.7 shows the ratio of consumption of the top 20% of incomes over the bottom 40% for different categories of services. In the case of private health, for instance, the top income quintile consumes 6.9 times what the bottom two quintiles consume; in the case of transport and communications, the top quintile consumes 5.3 times what the bottom 40% consume; and in the area of education, culture and leisure, the top 20% consume 4.9 times what the bottom 40% consume. Given the fact that the richer gain a lot more from exemptions, it could have been expected that the VAT burden on top income deciles would be even lower. The fact that the top income decile still faces an average VAT rate of 4.6% may suggest that rich households buy more but also more expensive taxed goods and services.

Figure 4.6. **Distribution of exemptions per income decile expressed as a % of GDP**

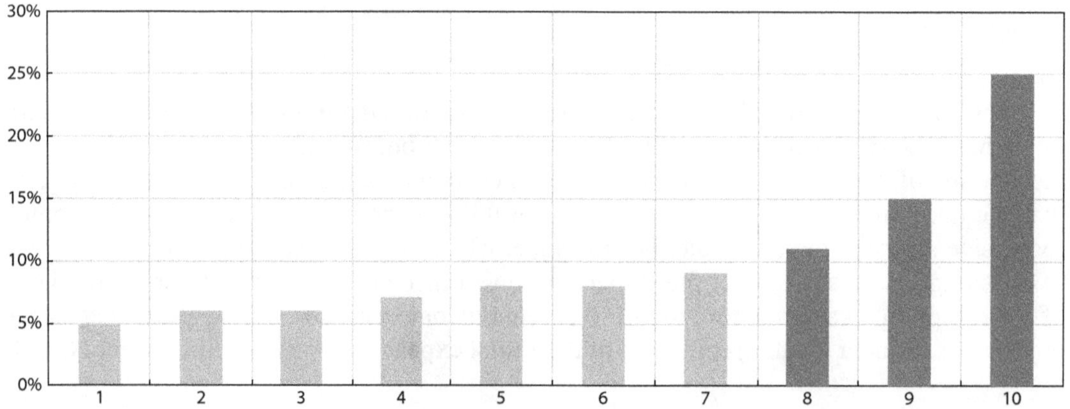

StatLink http://dx.doi.org/10.1787/888933545025

Source: Ministerio de Hacienda (2016).

Figure 4.7. **Ratio of consumption between the top 20% incomes and the lowest 40% incomes**

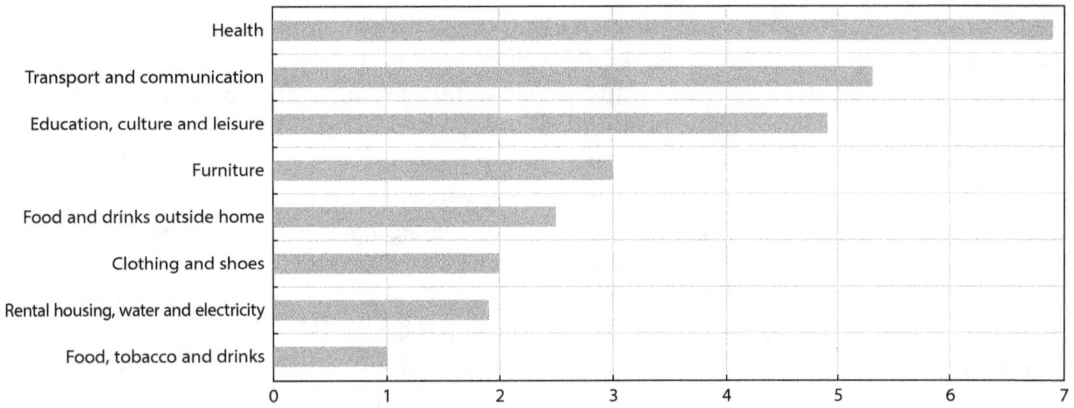

StatLink http://dx.doi.org/10.1787/888933545044

Source: Based on « Encuesta Ingresos y Gastos de los Hogares 2004 » in Garro et al. (2015).

Under the current reform proposal, a number of regressive exemptions would become subject to the 4% reduced VAT rate. The tax reform bill foresees a significant reduction in the number of exemptions, including a narrowing of the basic goods basket (*canasta básica*) and taxing private education services and health services, which are currently exempt, at the reduced VAT rate of 4%. While this is a step in the right direction, it is likely that those reduced VAT rates would continue to provide greater benefits to richer than to poorer households. Thus, further broadening the VAT base by removing additional exemptions and reduced VAT rates could be considered.

The wide use of zero-rating generates significant revenue losses as well as administrative costs

"Quasi" zero-rating is widely used under Costa Rica's sales tax. Under a regular VAT, businesses that sell exempt goods or services cannot recover input VAT and VAT becomes a cost for businesses. Therefore, standard advice is to limit the use of exemptions as much as possible as they violate the fundamental principles of a VAT. In order to prevent those distortions, goods – which are defined in Article 9 of the Sales Tax Law as exempt – are effectively "zero-rated", meaning that input sales tax, under a number of restrictions (see below), can be recovered by producers of exempt goods.

Allowing for the recovery of input VAT in the production of exempt supplies is very expensive in terms of revenue foregone and is hard to control. Zero-rating implies that a considerable amount of non-exempt goods sold in Costa Rica (i.e. the goods used as input in the production/ sale of exempt products) also escape taxation under the general sales tax. Hence, exemptions with a full right to input tax credit result both in a direct and indirect loss in general sales tax revenues. It should be mentioned as well that controlling the application of zero-rating is very difficult. For instance, excessive VAT refund claims, in particular through the use of fake invoices or by disguising sales as zero-rated sales, either under domestic zero-rating provisions or because goods are exported, is an issue that all countries face.

Because of the cost and administrative difficulties associated with zero-rating, producers of exempt goods and exporters can acquire inputs free of sales tax for authorised purchases (*compras autorizadas sin el pago de impuesto de ventas*).

Such a measure aims at reducing the volume of refund claims by businesses that sell predominately zero-rated outputs and that are therefore in a structural excess input-tax credit position. Such a system requires businesses to obtain an authorisation that allows their suppliers not to charge sales tax. However, this system may exacerbate the issue as opposed to addressing it. The business that supply products free of general sales tax to authorised producers of exempt goods and exporters retain the right to recover the associated input sales tax that they have incurred themselves. As a result, they might now end up in a refund position rather than the authorised producers of exempt goods and exporters. This means that the challenge of managing sales tax refunds is shifted from a limited number of often well-known producers of exempt goods and exporters to a potentially large number of downstream suppliers. This system is also open to abuse, in particular through false certificates. It is advised that Costa Rica considers phasing out this regime and implements a proper refund process within the context of its VAT reform. This should allow Costa Rica to organise the verification of refund claims within a wider risk-based tax compliance and administration framework.

A broad-based VAT system would address these issues at source. With the proposed tax reform, the recovery of input tax would be regulated by a new set of rules and the number of exemptions would be considerably decreased. VAT paid on inputs to produce exempt outputs would not be recoverable. This would go hand-in-hand with the removal of many exemptions. This would be a very welcome change. The main objective for Costa Rica should be to put in place a broad-based VAT system, with limited exemptions and zero rates. With a broad-based VAT system and timely VAT refunds, ensuring neutrality by effectively zero-rating exemptions would no longer be needed. VAT would be collected on final consumption and businesses would be able to fully recover input VAT.

Restrictions on the recovery of input sales tax generate distortions

Costa Rica imposes restrictions on taxpayers' rights to claim input tax credits. Indeed, the Costa Rican system only allows the deduction of input tax incurred on goods and certain services which are directly used in the manufacturing, marketing or distribution of taxable goods and in the provision of taxable services. This system also applies in the case of exempt goods. Until recently, the system for sales tax credits was even more restrictive as sales tax could only be recovered on the inputs that were physically incorporated into production and on the capital assets that were directly related to the production phase.

This treatment goes against the neutrality principle of a VAT which, in a domestic context, should be achieved by allowing suppliers a right to credit the input tax at each stage of the supply chain, so that the tax burden eventually lies on the final consumer rather than the intermediaries in the supply chain. This treatment increases the tax burden on final consumers through cascading effects, as unrecoverable sales tax will be (fully or partly) capitalised in prices of intermediate outputs and taxed again under the sales tax when products are sold. This results in a number of economic distortions including on input choices as it may induce producers to substitute away from those inputs and/or prefer exempt input suppliers and it may provide tax-induced incentives to change businesses structure (e.g. for vertical integration). It puts domestic businesses also at a competitive disadvantage compared to foreign businesses as the non-recoverable tax ends up being hidden in the cost of domestically produced goods and services. As a result, the non-recoverable sales tax forms part of the cost base of Costa Rican taxpayers' exports and generates a hidden tax on these exports.

The existing system also generates compliance and administrative costs. Determining whether taxpayers are entitled to credits requires differentiating between the goods and services that have directly been used in the manufacturing, marketing and distribution process and those which are not, such as overhead business expenses which cannot be deduced. Thus, a reform focusing on turning the current sales tax into a broad-based VAT should also involve removing restrictions on the recovery of input VAT for producers of taxable supplies to enhance neutrality and limit compliance and administrative costs.

Well-targeted transfers could mitigate the distributional effects of a broad-based VAT

As part of the VAT reform, the government has proposed the introduction of transfers to compensate the poorest households for the increase in VAT. The reform proposal follows the concept of "personalised VAT" which combines a broad-based VAT with transfers to the poorest taxpayers (Box 4.2). The proposed system would compensate households in the lowest three income deciles. As discussed above, such a system would avoid providing untargeted support to all consumers through exemptions or reduced rates.

In practice, the proposed transfer system would be innovative. Refunds would be granted per household, taking into account the number of individuals in each household. The amount of the transfers would be based on average consumption levels. The first decile would be compensated for the average consumption levels of the second and third deciles, while households in the second and third income deciles would be compensated for the average consumption levels in their respective deciles. This would increase the transfers' progressivity. The Ministry of Hacienda would transfer refunds electronically to consumers' bank accounts on a monthly basis, through the *Sistema Unico de Pago de Recurso Social*, based on the information that IMAS would provide using the *Sistema National de Informacion Social y Registro Unico de Beneficiarios.*

Alternative compensation mechanisms exist but might not necessarily reach the poor who work in the informal economy. A non-wasteable earned-income tax credit (EITC) would be an alternative measure that could compensate low-income households for the VAT base broadening and tax rate increase while providing also incentives to enter the formal economy. The EITC would lower the PIT liability and would be paid out as a cash transfer to households who have insufficient tax liability to claim the credit (see Chapter 3). Such an EITC would therefore constitute a double dividend. However, households who would continue to work in the informal economy would remain out of the reach of the credit, which would not be the case under the transfer system which Costa Rica is planning to implement.

The government expects that those transfers will significantly mitigate the regressivity of the VAT reform and contribute to reducing poverty. Figure 4.8 shows the distribution of tax payments expressed as a share of GDP across income deciles under the current sales tax and under the proposed VAT reform – both with and without the transfers. With the transfers, VAT payments would become negative for the first income decile and the second and third deciles would pay close to no VAT. Figure 4.9 shows that instead of experiencing increases in VAT payments with a shift from the current sales tax to a VAT system without transfers, introducing a VAT system with transfers would significantly reduce tax burdens for the lowest three income deciles. On the other hand, for households from the fourth to the last income deciles, the tax burden would increase slightly.

Box 4.2. **Personalised VAT**

The concept of personalised VAT was proposed by Barreix, Bès and Roca (2012) as a way of solving the "impossible trinity of VAT", according to which "No consumption tax has ever had all three of the critical attributes of a progressive consumption tax: a broad base, a single rate and measured relief for those in greatest need" (Ainsworth, 2006).

Simply put, personalised VAT consists in:

- *Broadening the tax base.* The only exemptions which will be kept are those which make sense from the tax administration's point of view and/or those cases which are necessary in order to ensure consistency in the tax treatment of similar concepts.
- *Unifying the tax rate.* This recommendation is consistent with best practices and fundamentally responds to the need to simplify the tax administration and obtain greater neutrality.
- *Providing tax relief to individuals in the lowest income deciles.* This requires two kinds of actions: determining the amount of relief to be granted and identifying the individuals who will be awarded this relief. The term "personalised" stems from the fact that the proposal seeks to compensate the tax impact on the consumption of an average person belonging to the decile which we are seeking to provide tax relief.

Source: "Solving the Impossible Trinity of Consumption Taxes Personalized VAT", Barreix et al. (2012).

Figure 4.8. **Distribution of tax payments expressed as a share of GDP across income deciles under the current sales tax and the proposed VAT reform**

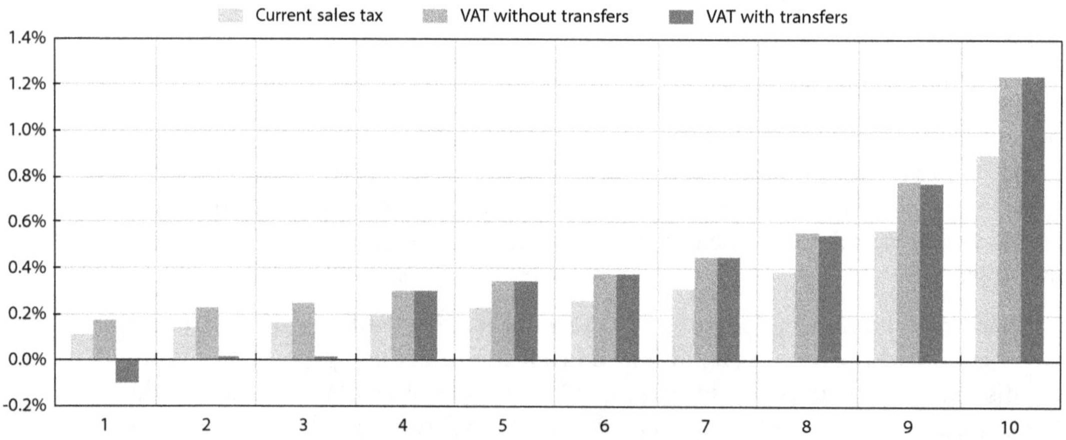

StatLink http://dx.doi.org/10.1787/888933545063

Source: Based on data from Ministerio de Hacienda (2017).

Figure 4.9. **Percentage change in VAT payments across income deciles with and without transfers**

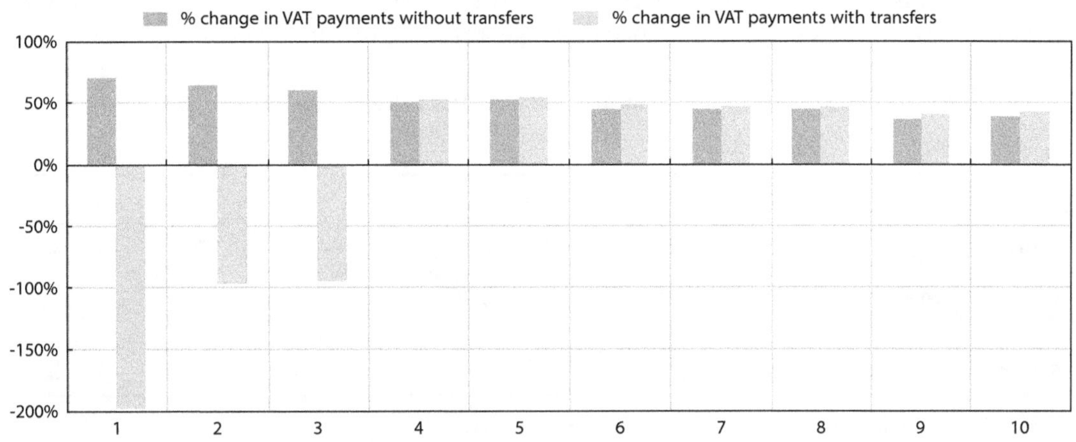

StatLink http://dx.doi.org/10.1787/888933545082

Source: Based on data from Ministerio de Hacienda (2017).

However, these projections are based on the assumption that the transfer system will function well, which may be challenging in practice. The major difficulty will be to ensure that the system effectively reaches the poor. The poorest households tend to live in rural areas and are often not part of the formal economy or formal labour force. If the system does not reach a sufficient share of poor households, it is estimated that the system could have undesired effects on poverty and inequality reduction. Thus, the necessary condition for the system to effectively compensate the poor will be to ensure the easy receipt of the benefit through a simple and accessible granting system. Another challenge will be to ensure that households qualifying and ultimately benefiting from the transfers are not households that hide their income or households that may be income-poor but asset-rich. This issue should be addressed through information cross-checking, in particular with the tax administration, to verify that the information on the beneficiaries of transfers matches the tax administration's information.

The cash-transfer system would allow the government to broaden the VAT base significantly. As poor households would be compensated for the VAT they pay, the government could start levying VAT on basic goods and services, such as the goods included in the basic consumption basket (*canasta básica*), agricultural inputs, the monthly consumption of electric energy, etc. Even if the government preferred to postpone such a reform until the cash-transfer system is fully operational and has proven to be effective in reaching all poor households, there are advantages to already including those measures in the current VAT reform. Broadening the VAT base to basic goods could be made conditional upon the realisation of certain objectives, such as the degree to which the compensation mechanism turns out to be effective in reaching poor households.

Sales tax evasion is high

Sales tax evasion is relatively high. Non tax compliance can be calculated as the difference between the revenues that would have been collected if the sales tax had been perfectly enforced (theoretical revenues, *Rt*) and the revenues that were actually collected (actual revenues, *Ra*). Based on data from the Ministry of Hacienda, Table 4.1 measures the revenue loss from tax non-compliance, calculated as *(Rt - Ra)/Rt*. In 2013, non-tax compliance cost about a fifth of potential sales tax revenues. Table 4.1 also shows that sales tax evasion was relatively stable between 2010 and 2013. Those results suggest that measures to promote greater sales tax compliance could generate significant revenue increases.

Table 4.1. **Revenue losses from non-compliance with the sales tax as a share of GDP between 2010 and 2013**

	2010	2011	2012	2013
Actual tax collection (CRC million) (*Ra*)	920 298	1 029 811	1 122 978	1 176 745
Theoretical revenues with perfect enforcement of the sales tax (CRC million) (*Rt*)	1 152 927	1 263 876	1 384 375	1 468 182
Revenue loss from non-compliance (%) (*Rt - Ra*)/*Rt*	20.2%	18.5%	18.9%	19.9%

Source: Based on data from Dirección General de Hacienda (2015).

To address tax avoidance and fraud, the tax administration has implemented a mechanism which requires entities that process credit or debit card payments to act as withholding agents. The withholding rate is up to 6% of the net amount paid. It is an advance payment of the sales tax that is withheld by the credit or debit cards companies from the sales price paid by the customer and that is remitted directly to the Treasury. This mechanism reduces the amount of tax revenue at stake and allows the tax administration cross information concerning sales and purchases. The tax administration compares sales tax forms with income tax forms to detect transactions that are not reported by any of the parties and imposes sanctions. To effectively tackle tax fraud, Costa Rica should also implement a modern risk-based tax compliance management model, which includes the effective use of technologies to facilitate compliance for taxpayers that are willing to comply and to boost enforcement capacities to deal with taxpayers that are unwilling to comply.

A broader-based and better administered VAT could also contribute to reducing informality

VAT can help collect revenues from the informal sector. As mentioned previously, informality is a significant issue in Costa Rica. The simplest way to tax the informal sector is through indirect taxes, by taxing the goods and services that informal businesses buy and sell (Joshi et al., 2014). VAT increases the tax burden on the informal sector as informal businesses might have to pay at least some VAT on their inputs but would not be entitled to VAT refunds. This does not require any active informal sector participation in the tax system (e.g. filing tax returns) and thus does not involve compliance costs issues (Joshi et al., 2014). VAT functions in part as a tax on the purchases of informal operators from formal sector businesses (Keen, 2007).

In addition to being able to tax a wide range of economic activities, VAT theoretically creates positive "chain" effects incentivising economic agents to become formal. An important benefit of VAT is that it can create positive incentives for informal sector firms with actual or prospective dealings with formal sector firms to enter the formal tax system in order to be able to claim tax credits and recover their input VAT. A recent study of small firms in Brazil shows that an individual firm is more likely to register for VAT if its suppliers and/or customers are registered (de Paula and Scheinkman, 2010).

Additional incentives and dissuasive measures are important to reduce informality. As opposed to many OECD countries, Costa Rica does not exempt suppliers under a minimum turnover threshold from the requirement to register for and/or collect sales tax; sales tax is mandatory for all businesses. In general, VAT registration thresholds are put in place to lower compliance costs for small businesses, lower tax administration costs, and ensure a more effective use of administrative resources and audit capacity. Costa Rica could weigh the possible advantages of introducing a registration threshold against potential disadvantages (e.g. loss in tax revenues, tax discrimination between exempt and taxable firms, risk of fraud and incentives to stay below the threshold). Other typical measures to support formalisation include simplified VAT registration procedures for small businesses, which Costa Rica has.

VAT rules on cross-border trade in services still need to be aligned with the OECD VAT/GST Guidelines

The OECD Council adopted a Recommendation in September 2016 that incorporates internationally agreed guidelines for the consistent application of VAT to cross-border trade. These International OECD VAT/GST Guidelines (OECD, 2017) present a set of fundamental principles for the design and operation of VAT systems and their application to cross-border transactions (Box 4.3).

Box 4.3. The OECD International VAT/GST Guidelines

At the November 2015 OECD Global Forum on VAT, more than 100 countries and jurisdictions endorsed the OECD International VAT/GST Guidelines as the international standard to ensure a coherent and efficient application of VAT/GST to international trade in services. These Guidelines were incorporated into a Recommendation that was adopted by the OECD Council in September 2016.

In the absence of these Guidelines, there was no internationally agreed framework for the application of VAT to cross-border trade, in contrast with existing frameworks for the taxation of income such as the OECD Model Tax Convention and the Transfer Pricing Guidelines. This led to increasing uncertainty and complexity for both tax authorities and businesses and risks of double taxation and unintended non-taxation. This was a matter of special concern with respect to international trade in services and intangibles, which has considerably increased over the last decade.

The Guidelines include chapters on the principle of VAT neutrality and its implementation in practice, and on the implementation of the destination principle for allocating the taxing rights on cross-border supplies of services and intangibles.

For business-to-business supplies the Guidelines establish that, the taxing rights on cross-border supplies of services and intangibles are to be allocated to the jurisdiction where the business customer has located its permanent business presence. For business-to-consumer supplies, the Guidelines recommend that the taxing rights over "on-the-spot supplies" be allocated to the jurisdiction in which the supply is physically performed; and that the taxing rights over all other supplies and services be allocated to the jurisdiction in which the customer has its usual residence. These include remote supplies of services and digital products over the Internet (e.g. apps, streaming of music and movies, online gaming) by foreign suppliers. The Guidelines recommend that these foreign suppliers be required to register and remit VAT in the jurisdiction of taxation and that countries implement a simplified registration and compliance regime to facilitate compliance for non-resident suppliers.

Box 4.3. **The OECD International VAT/GST Guidelines** *(continued)*

The Guidelines do not aim at providing detailed prescriptions for national legislation. Jurisdictions are sovereign with respect to the design and application of their laws. Rather, the Guidelines seek to identify objectives and suggest means for achieving them, thereby serving as a reference point. Global Forum participants urged the OECD and G20 to develop implementation packages to support the consistent implementation of the Guidelines and to design an even more inclusive framework that would involve all interested countries and jurisdictions, particularly developing countries, on an equal footing.

As mentioned previously, Costa Rica's sales tax system is currently not in line with the key international principle of neutrality as promoted by the OECD International VAT/GST Guidelines, which has a number of dimensions including the absence of discrimination and the elimination of undue tax burdens and disproportionate or inappropriate compliance costs for businesses. The planned VAT reform aims at implementing a broad-based VAT regime that will be aligned with the international principles of neutrality and destination as promoted by the Guidelines

The draft VAT bill intends to tax the supply of services to Costa Rican customers by foreign suppliers ("inbound services"), by requiring credit and debit card companies to collect the VAT on these purchases. Services supplied by a non-resident business to a customer in Costa Rica would be subject to VAT if the recipient is tax-resident in Costa Rica. In practice, the draft bill would require public and private credit and debit card companies (usually a bank or financial institution) to act as perception agent and levy the VAT every time their cardholders purchase goods, intangibles and services through the Internet or any other telecommunications platform. For every international internet transaction, the debit/credit card company would charge the corresponding VAT rate and cardholders would receive an additional charge on their card statements reflecting the collection of VAT.

In practice, credit or debit card companies receive information about where transactions take place from credit card networks (MasterCard, Visa, AMEX and Discover are the four major credit card networks). When a cardholder purchases something in a national or international marketplace the credit card network tracks the information and verifies the transaction with the card company, which then approves the transaction and charges the cardholder. The proposal also contains a provision for cases like PayPal, which can be traded through an online bank account to make payments to the account of a non-resident supplier for goods, services or intangibles, making these transactions taxable.

In certain situations, the tax administration would reimburse the tax collected to the cardholder: (1) purchases of intangible goods and services through the Internet if they are used or consumed in another jurisdiction; (2) purchases of online goods for which VAT is charged at customs, which might cause double taxation; (3) use of electronic payment methods for money transfers to persons or entities located abroad for personal care or final consumption in a different jurisdiction than Costa Rica; and (4) purchases of goods or services exempted by law. In the above scenarios, the burden of proof would lie with the cardholder. The tax administration would then cross information with the debit/credit card company before reimbursing VAT.

There are a number of technical difficulties, however, that could limit the system's effectiveness. Costa Rica would need to ensure that its system for collecting VAT on supplies of services and intangibles by non-resident suppliers functions properly to be consistent with the VAT/GST Guidelines. However, technical difficulties may arise. The first main technical difficulty is that there are alternative ways of purchasing goods or services online. Another technical challenge is that banks, in addition to the costs associated with the implementation of this system, might need time to develop the system to be able to implement these regulations.

The tax policy recommendations that can be drawn from this analysis are as follows:

Recommendations

- Implement a comprehensive reform to convert the existing sales tax into a modern VAT with a broad base which includes services
- Consider further narrowing exemptions for goods and services that are primarily consumed by high-income individuals; continue broadening the VAT base when the compensation mechanism has become effective in reaching poor households.
- Gradually raise the standard VAT rate
- Compensate low-income households for increases in VAT through easily accessible transfers
- Move towards a full VAT credit system
- Implement a modern risk-based tax compliance administration strategy
- Implement an efficient and effective mechanism for the collection of VAT on inbound B2C services from foreign suppliers
- Align its VAT with the neutrality and destination principles promoted by the OECD International VAT/GST Guidelines

References

Barreix A., M. Bès, and J. Roca (2012), "Solving the impossible trinity of consumption taxes: personalized VAT", *Fiscal Reform in Latin America*, ECLAC; CIDOB Foundation, Santiago, LC/L.3522, p. 49-77.

de Paula, A. and J. Scheinkman (2010), "Value-added taxes, chain effects, and informality", *American Economic Journal: Macroeconomics*, 2, 195–221.

Dirección General de Hacienda (2015), *Incumplimiento Tributario en Impuestos sobre la Renta y Ventas 2010-2013*, [Non-compliance with income taxes and sales tax 2010-2013], San José de Costa Rica.

Joshi, A., W. Pritchard and C. Heady (2014), "Taxing the informal economy: the current state of knowledge and agendas for future Research", *The Journal of Development Studies*, Vol. 50, No. 10, p. 1325-1347

Keen, M. (2007), "VAT, tariffs, and withholding: border taxes and informality in developing countries", *IMF Working Paper*, WP/ 07/174, Washington, DC.

OECD (2017), *International VAT/GST Guidelines*, OECD Publishing, Paris, http://dx.doi.org/10.1787/9789264271401-en.

OECD (2010), *Tax Policy Reform and Economic Growth*, OECD Publishing, Paris, http://dx.doi.org/10.1787/9789264091085-en.

OECD/KIPF (2014), *The Distributional Effects of Consumption Taxes in OECD Countries*, OECD Publishing, Paris, http://dx.doi.org/10.1787/9789264224520-en.

Rodríguez Garro F., F. Sancho Mora and R. Fonseca Hernández (2015), "Bases para un sistema tributario progresivo en Costa Rica", [Basis for a progressive tax system in Costa Rica], Revista Pensamiento Actual, Vol. 15, No. 24, 2015 – Universidad de Costa Rica – Sede de Occidente.

Chapter 5

Using tax policy to address Costa Rica's domestic environmental challenges

This chapter discusses environmentally related taxes in Costa Rica, and some broader tax provisions that influence environmental outcomes. The chapter discusses how the environmental effectiveness of taxation can be improved while tax revenues can be increased. The chapter analyses the design of the fuel tax and discusses whether its rates could be better aligned with the external costs of fuel use. The sales and import tax exemptions for fuels translate into a de facto preferential treatment of fuels compared to other products. Costa Rica's vehicle taxes are discussed, and the chapter suggests how they could be modified to better align with environmental policy objectives. In addition, the chapter comments on the differential taxation of private and public electricity producers, the recent initiative for a tax on non-reusable plastic containers, and the cost-effectiveness of the country's Payments for Environmental Services Programme.

Reaching ambitious domestic environmental and climate policy objectives will require addressing existing and emerging challenges

Costa Rica has put forward an ambitious climate policy agenda, and promotes itself as an environmental and climate policy forerunner. The 2011 National Climate Strategy (Ministry of Environment – MINAE, 2011) commits the country to achieve carbon neutrality by 2021. This target allows Costa Rica to compensate its emissions through forests, so that total net emissions in 2021 are comparable to total emissions in 2005 (MINAE, 2015). The target included in the recent Nationally Determined Contribution (NDC), which applies in parallel, puts forward that Costa Rica will keep net greenhouse gas (GHG) emissions below 9.37 $MtCO_2e$ by 2030, including carbon removals through forests (MINAE, 2015). The domestic target to generate 100% of electricity from renewables is also worth highlighting (MINAE, 2015), though almost 100% of electricity has already been generated from renewables in the past years. Changes to tax policies proposed for 2017, but also some reforms that go beyond those already suggested, can help achieve these goals. In addition, the National Energy Plan (MINAE, 2014a) outlines important measures to achieve low-carbon development in Costa Rica by 2030, in line with the domestic targets for climate policies.

Per-capita emissions in Costa Rica remain low, but additional policies are needed to reach domestic climate policy goals. When including carbon removals from forests, total domestic GHG emissions have been relatively stable between 1990 and 2010, but emissions doubled from 6 $MtCO_2e$ in 1990 to 12 $MtCO_2e$ in 2010 when excluding removals through carbon sinks (Climate Action Tracker, 2015). Though carbon emissions per capita remain low when compared to the OECD average and Latin American OECD members, containing the rapid emissions growth especially in transport, but also in agriculture, waste, industry and the residential sector will be key to reach Costa Rica's ambitious climate policy targets.

The transport sector is the largest polluter, and also contributes significantly to local air pollution and congestion. Of the GHG emissions from the energy sector (39% of total GHG), transport accounts for the large majority (68.7%), and they are increasing rapidly. Beyond the sector's contribution to climate change, it also causes local air pollution, which increases the burden of disease in many countries (WHO, 2016; OECD, 2016b). In Costa Rica, air pollution is concentrated around the San José Greater Metropolitan Area, where almost two-thirds of the population lives (Ministry of Health, 2015; Granoff et al., 2015). The large and fast growth in the number of private cars (by 68% between 2003 and 2014) and other vehicles drives the increase in air pollution around the capital. Private cars account for 41% of emissions from road transport, followed by heavy transport (22%) and two-wheelers (16%) (MINAE, 2014a). The old age of vehicles, and thus of the motor technology, amplifies emissions per kilometre driven (ibid.). In addition, the large number of vehicles leads to high traffic congestion in the capital, in response to which driving restrictions have been in place since 2005.

The low carbon-intensity of electricity generation is impressive, but climatic factors threaten the country's high reliance on hydro-electricity. Electricity is almost exclusively generated from emissions-free sources, which are supplemented by thermal generation from fossil fuels when necessary. This is a remarkable achievement given the high shares of GHG emissions from the electricity generation worldwide. While the generation mix varies from year to year according to climatic factors, electricity is predominantly generated from hydro (up to 80%), followed by geothermal (around 15%), wind (up to 10%) and much smaller proportions of solar and biomass. However, droughts, and other environmental challenges put the country's high reliance on hydro-electricity at risk (Ministry of Environment, 2014a; OECD, 2016). Other economic sectors account for much smaller shares of emissions, and a more detailed discussion of their emissions profile is outside of the scope of this chapter.[1]

Tax policy can help address Costa Rica's environmental challenges in the transport and electricity sectors. Taxes often are levied to raise government revenue, and where this is their principal objective, behavioural responses by taxpayers are usually undesirable. In other cases, including environmental taxation, changing behaviour (to discourage harmful behaviours) can be a policy objective. Environmentally-related taxes are not levied for environmental reasons alone, but they can be effective instruments for pursuing environmental objectives, e.g. emissions reductions (Box 5.1). However, next to core environmental and climate policies, the broader tax policy framework needs to be aligned with environmental and climate policy objectives (OECD, 2015b). For example, the VAT, the corporate income tax or taxes on immovable property may affect choices around energy consumption, investment and mobility, and as result these taxes are discussed in this chapter where they interact with environmentally-related taxes and environmental policy objectives.

This chapter focuses on the role of tax policy in the electricity and transport sectors, and also includes brief comment on the initiative to introduce a tax on plastic containers and on the Payments for Environmental Services Programme. Other environmental challenges, such as the lack of public facilities for wastewater management, the high intensity of fertilizer use by agriculture, and management of fisheries are described in more detail in Granoff et al. (2015), but are outside of the scope of this chapter. The Costa Rican charges on water and mining are also not discussed here.

Revenues from environmentally-related taxes are relatively high

Environmentally-related tax revenue as a share of GDP is relatively high in comparison with OECD and other Latin American countries. The OECD defines environmentally-related taxes as any tax levied on environmentally-relevant tax-bases, such as air or water, energy sources or motor vehicles, regardless of the reason why they were introduced. In Costa Rica, the revenue raised from these taxes is in the order of magnitude of 2.2 % of GDP in 2014, compared to 2% on average across the OECD and selected partner economies (Figure 5.1). As in most countries, a major part of these revenues is from energy taxes (1.5% of GDP) and taxes on motor vehicles (0.7% when compared to GDP). Revenues from charges on water consumption are much lower (0.01% of GDP).

High levels of environmentally related tax revenues require careful interpretation before strong policy conclusions can be drawn. High environmentally-related tax revenues (as a percentage of GDP) could be seen as a measure of success in the sense that they indicate more attention for environment policy using taxes. They could, however, also point to weakness since high revenues could indicate high remaining pollution. Most analyses emphasise the first interpretation, i.e. taking higher revenue shares as mainly indicative of stronger effort. Based on the trends in the growth of road transport in Costa Rica, as outlined earlier, the base for fuel and motor vehicle taxes could substantially increase in the next years. In the case of Costa Rica, the second interpretation could thus merit more emphasis, in particular going forward. At the same time, raising revenues is a legitimate reason for introducing, aligning or increasing the rates of environmentally related taxes, but it is crucial to take account of the behavioural incentives in tax design as well.

Figure 5.1. **Revenues from environmentally related taxes as a % of GDP**

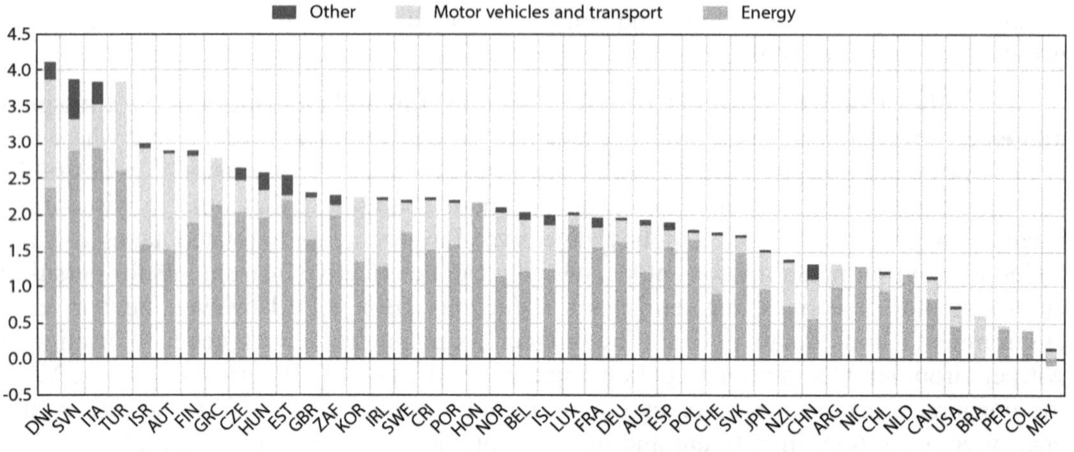

StatLink http://dx.doi.org/10.1787/888933545101

Source: OECD Database on Instruments Used for Environmental Policy.

Costa Rica could consider reviewing its practice of earmarking the revenues from environmentally-related taxes. Revenues from environmentally-related taxes, more often than other taxes, are subject to multiple claims on their use. For example, it is often discussed to employ the proceeds from proposed carbon taxes or emissions trading systems to finance public or private investment into low-carbon infrastructure, use it to reach internationals goals for climate finance, or finance other specific purposes, such as funds to invest into environmental improvements. As discussed in chapter 1, earmarking the proceeds of environmentally-related taxes for specific environmental funds is relatively prevalent in Costa Rica, and imbalances between revenue-raising and spending proceeds occur frequently. In general, public finance theory and practice tends to discourage strict legal earmarking of the revenues of a particular tax or revenue-raising instrument, as they are unlikely to map very closely to the appropriate or desired levels of government spending on a particular policy area. While it can often be easier to justify the introduction of environmentally-related taxes on the grounds of earmarking their proceeds, Costa Rica may want to review this practice to increase the flexibility of attending to specific financing needs and priorities.

Box 5.1. **Why taxes are among the best environmental policy instruments**

The environmental, health and climate impacts (in short, pollution) of energy use are not directly borne by producers and consumers, so these costs are not taken into account in decisions based on market prices: they are external to the market. The result is that unregulated market outcomes lead to too much pollution, and public policy is needed to improve upon the market outcome by reducing pollution. Governments can intervene with various policy instruments, including taxes, cap-and-trade systems (tradable permits), emission standards, direct technology requirements and restricting the level of pollution-generating activity.

Taxes or auctioned tradable permits tend to outperform other environmental policy instruments in terms of cost-effectiveness. This is because putting a price on pollution provides polluters with incentives to find the cheapest ways of reducing their tax bill. They can reduce the level of the pollution-generating activity or search for less pollution-intensive

Box 5.1. **Why taxes are among the best environmental policy instruments** *(continued)*

ways of carrying it out. Alternative instruments, for example energy efficiency standards, imply more prescriptive policy decisions on how to reduce pollution, and given asymmetrical information and heterogeneity among economic agents, the proposed solutions risk not being cost-effective. Polluters possess more information than the government about how they can cut pollution, so they are better placed to choose the cheapest option. Since economic agents differ, the best options can differ as well. For example, some households would be better off by responding to a higher fuel tax by investing in more fuel efficient cars, whereas others would primarily respond by driving less. A fuel economy standard, however, would force the second household to (also) invest in fuel economy, even though this would not be their preferred response. Furthermore, once polluters comply with an energy efficiency standard, they do not have an incentive to further reduce pollution, whereas with a tax the incentive to cut pollution is on-going.

Market-based instruments have strong appeal on theoretical grounds and there is evidence that they often work better in practice than other policy instruments (see e.g. OECD, 2013a). Nevertheless, direct regulation, for example with efficiency or emission standards, can be useful in particular circumstances, either in combination with market-based instruments or instead of them. One complication with the use of taxes is that it may be difficult to tax pollution directly and that taxes have to be levied on activities or types of consumption that are more or less strongly related to pollution. When the correlation is weak, taxes become less effective and the relative appeal of direct regulation rises. Fuel taxes, for example, can very accurately reflect the carbon content of fuels and therefore the marginal contribution of fuel use to climate costs, but they correlate less directly with emissions of local pollutants and still less with the ultimate pollution costs resulting from such emissions. Emission standards for local pollutants can usefully complement fuel taxes, but the case for fuel economy standards is weaker. Furthermore, designing effective emission standards is not easy, with e.g. the risk that emission profiles differ substantially between test- and real-world conditions. Using standards to cut pollution is also more likely to work well in the early stages of abatement, when pollution is high and cheap technological approaches to reduce it are available. Market-based approaches become more attractive when abatement costs rise and across-the-board measures should make way for more decentralised abatement choices.

Source: OECD (2015a).

There is scope to adapt the policy mix to curb the external costs from road transport in Costa Rica

Pricing road externalities can help contain the external costs of road transport. There is a wide range of external costs from road transport: some of the main externalities for which measurement has been attempted include climate change, local air pollution, traffic congestion, and road damage (Van Dender and Parry, forthcoming). Ideally, the different nature and sources of each of these externalities would require its own policy instrument, but practical solutions exist and are used in a range of countries (Table 5.1).

Costa Rica operates a number of tax instruments which could be adapted to better address the negative side effects of road transport. These instruments – irrespective of the precise motivation for their introduction and design – can be loosely mapped to the different externalities from road transport. For example, the Costa Rican fuel tax can be thought of as an attempt to address the contribution of fuel use to climate change, though the Costa Rican specific tax rates do not map very closely to the GHG content of the underlying fuels. Furthermore, the reduction of the vehicle tax for electric and hybrid vehicles can be interpreted as an attempt to reduce air pollution, but, as explained further down, this type of tax differentiation is not the first choice to influence the emissions profile of the vehicle fleet. While it is difficult to quantify the relative importance of the different external costs of road transport in the Costa Rican context, a range of changes to the existing tax policy framework could help target these costs more precisely. This can be expected to result in reducing pollution and other undesirable side effects of transport.

Table 5.1. **Ideal and practical policies to address the external costs of road transport**

Externality	Cause	Ideal policy	Most practical policy	Countries with similar policies
Climate change	Fuel use emits carbon and other GHG, emissions, roughly proportionate to the amount of fuel combusted	Fuel tax	Fuel tax	All OECD and G20 economies, and beyond
Air pollution	Fuel use produces air pollution, either through combustion directly, or indirectly through reactions with ambient air	Tax tailpipe emissions per vehicle kilometre, with rates varying proportionally to local population exposure, topography, weather, interaction with other pollutants and ultimate pollution impact	Driving-based charge with component to reflect air pollution cost. Fuel tax to reflect differences in pollution profiles between fuels or to substitute for driving-based charge.	Distance-based charges for trucks in some EU countries.
Congestion	Drivers do not account for the road space used by their vehicle, which leads to congested roads and may raise travel time and reduce travel time reliability for all vehicles	Per-kilometre charges for vehicles driven on busy roads, with charges aligned across roads and time of day with marginal external costs	Bottom-up pricing schemes (e.g. local cordon fees) Top-down pricing schemes (e.g. country-wide systems)	Cordon fees in Singapore, London, Milan, Stockholm, and others
Accidents	Drivers are not charged for the risks their extra driving poses to others	Per-kilometre tax, with rates scaled to the driver risk (e.g. on ratings from insurance companies accounting for age, prior crash record, etc.) and vehicle risks (heavier vehicles pose higher risks to other vehicle occupants).	Pay-as-you-drive (PAYD) insurance, with payments in proportion to km driven	PAYD system in Norway, Japan, Australia and others
Road damage	Driving causes road wear, mostly caused by trucks in relation to axle load	Per-kilometre tolls on heavy trucks, scaled by axle weight, ideally with higher rates for driving on more vulnerable road classes		Tolls for heavy vehicles in several EU countries, Switzerland, New Zealand

Source: Van Dender and Parry (forthcoming).

The fuel tax prices oil products at relatively high rates but the carbon content of underlying fuels is taxed at differing rates

Costa Rica levies a fuel tax on oil products but statutory rates differ across fuels. Costa Rica's fuel tax ("Impuesto Unico sobre los Combustibles") applies to most oil products used in the country. As in all OECD and G20 economies, taxes on fuels used in road transport are higher than the taxes on fuels used in other economic sectors (OECD, 2016). This is because, in the absence of more targeted policy instruments, taxes on transport fuels are often thought of as also addressing other externalities from road transport (Table 5.1). In contrast to practice in some other countries, which apply surcharges to fuel used for transport purposes to increase taxes on road fuels compared to fuel tax rates in other sectors, the differentiation in Costa Rica is not explicit and rather a result of higher taxes rates on gasoline and diesel, which are predominantly used in transport. Of the transport fuels, the highest rate is levied on super gasoline (CRC 245.5 per litre), and a slightly lower rate on regular gasoline (CRC 234.7 per litre). Diesel is taxed at a much lower rate (CRC 138.75 per litre). LPG, kerosene, fuel oil, bunker fuel and naphtha, which are predominantly used in the residential and industry sectors, and to a minor extent to generate electricity, are all taxed at rates substantially below the rates applied to road transport fuels (CRC 50 per litre). Fisheries are tax exempt, as are fuels used in international aviation and shipping, in line with international agreements. Natural gas and coal are not subject to the fuel tax. Natural gas and coal are not currently used much in Costa Rica, but this could change if the share of hydro to generate electricity were to decrease (see OECD, 2016 and above).

Where energy use is taxed, the tax rates in Costa Rica translate into relatively high effective tax rates on carbon. Figure 5.2 plots the rates of the fuel tax (on the vertical axis), as they applied on 1 April 2017, against carbon emissions from energy use in thousand tonnes of CO_2 (on the horizontal axis). Carbon emissions from energy use are divided by three economic sectors (transport, heating and process use, and fuels used to generate electricity). Figure 5.2 permits appreciating differences in the taxation of different fuels and sectors across the economy. Fuels used in transport (i.e. mostly gasoline and diesel) are taxed at the highest rates, while fuels used for heating and process purposes are taxed at much lower rates. Box 5.2 gives further detail on the interpretation of Figure 5.2, and provides background on OECD analyses of energy use and taxation in OECD and G20 economies.

The Costa Rican fuel tax prices carbon emissions at relatively high levels, also when compared to effective tax rates on energy use in OECD and G20 economies (see OECD, 2015a; OECD, 2016b for a full cross-country analysis of effective tax rates by fuel and sector). More specifically, the Costa Rican fuel tax translates into relatively high effective tax rates on carbon emissions. OECD (2016b) has chosen EUR 30 per tCO_2 as a *minimum* benchmark for the climate cost of carbon. Figure 5.2 shows that, where it applies, the Costa Rican fuel tax prices carbon emissions from energy use at rates which exceed EUR 30 per tCO_2 by far. This benchmark for the climate cost of carbon has been chosen as a lower-end reference for carbon prices. Selecting this lower-end estimate as a benchmark does not imply that carbon prices are sufficiently high at EUR 30 per tCO_2, and this is not a policy conclusion that should be drawn from this comparison. In addition, in contrast to practice in most OECD and G20 economies, the sales tax exemptions for fuels that exist in Costa Rica introduce strong variation in the relative prices of fuels in Costa Rica. However, taxes that usually apply to a very broad range of goods (such as value added and retail sales taxes) are not included in the graphical profiles. The *de facto* specific incidence of the Costa Rican sales tax on fuel prices complicates direct comparison of effective tax rates on fuels in Costa Rica with effective tax rates on fuels and sectors in other countries (see also Box 5.2, and the discussion some paragraphs further down).

Box 5.2. **Analysing taxes on energy use in Costa Rica, OECD and G20 countries**

The OECD has published detailed analyses of the taxation of energy use in OECD and G20 countries in *Taxing Energy Use: A Graphical Analysis* (OECD, 2013) and *Taxing Energy Use 2015: OECD and Selected Partner Economies* (OECD, 2015a). A key component of these analyses are the graphical profiles of energy use and taxation, which are prepared for each country included in the *Taxing Energy Use* database ("TEU database"), which contains comprehensive information on the rates and coverage of carbon and other specific energy taxes on energy use. Such a graphical profile of energy use and taxation (Figure 5.2) has been prepared for the purposes of this first OECD Tax Policy Review for Costa Rica. Figure 5.2 shows the composition of energy use in Costa Rica, and the effective rate of tax on various types of energy use.

The horizontal axis of each graphical profile shows all final use of energy by businesses and individuals, including the net energy used in energy transmission and in the transformation of energy from one form to another (e.g. crude oil to gasoline, coal to electricity). Energy use has been grouped into three broad categories: transport, heating and process use, and electricity. These three categories are further disaggregated for each country, generally reflecting the particular tax bases of that country. The subcategories therefore differ between countries depending on the nature of the fuel, its user, or its use.

All forms of energy are converted into common units of carbon emissions (tonnes of CO_2), using standard conversion factors. Figure 5.2 expresses the quantities of the various energy sources in terms of the carbon emissions associated with their use (in tonnes of CO_2). The re-expression of tax bases in terms of carbon content permits a focus on the structure of taxation with respect to one purpose for which fuel can be taxed – to reflect the social cost of carbon emissions. Electricity is different from most of the other energy types shown in that it is a secondary energy product which must be generated by use of some primary energy (e.g. coal, natural gas, nuclear power, and hydro). The electricity category of the graphical profiles therefore show the energy content or carbon emissions of the underlying primary fuels used to generate the electricity domestically rather than of the electricity itself. Data on energy use is taken from the Extended World Energy Balances (IEA, 2014).

On the vertical axis, Figure 5.2 shows the Costa Rican excise tax on fuels ("Impuesto Unico sobre los Combustibles") as at 1 April 2017. OECD analyses of energy use and taxation covers those taxes levied on a physical measure of energy product consumed, whether quoted in a monetary amount per unit of fuel (per-unit taxes), or as a percentage of the sales price (ad valorem taxes). In Costa Rica, the excise tax on fuels is quoted on a per-unit basis, in line with practice in most other countries.

Taxes that apply to a very broad range of goods (such as value added and retail sales taxes) are not included in the graphical profiles. Since these taxes usual apply at equal rates to a wide range of goods, they do not change relative prices. However, where an energy product is subject, for example, to a concessionary rate of VAT, the concession would affect relative prices. In order to gauge to what extent VAT rate differentiation takes place for energy products, OECD (2015) discusses VAT and concessionary VAT rates on energy products separately. Also excluded from the analysis are taxes that that may be related to energy use but that are not imposed directly on the energy product (such as vehicle taxes, road user charges or billing charges and taxes on emissions such as NO_X and SO_X) and those which do not have a fixed relationship to fuel volume (e.g. congestion charges).

The OECD also analyses *Effective Carbon Rates* (OECD, 2016b), defined as the total price that applies to CO_2 emissions from energy use as a result of market-based policy instruments. Compared to effective tax rates on carbon emissions from energy use, *Effective Carbon Rates* also include price signals from taxes and tradable emission permit prices. However, since Costa Rica does not operate a tradable permit system for carbon emissions, its effective tax rate on carbon emissions from energy use equals the effective carbon rate.

Source: adapted from OECD (2015b).

The tax rate on diesel could be increased at least to the level of the tax rate on gasoline, to reflect better the impact of diesel on climate change and air pollution. While gasoline is taxed at the highest rate in terms of the fuels' carbon content (Figure 5.2 shows the weighted average of the rates on premium and regular gasoline), diesel is taxed at a much lower effective tax rate on carbon. However, at current state of equipment and technology, diesel emits higher levels of harmful air pollutants per litre than gasoline (Harding, 2014), and the carbon content of diesel per litre is also higher than that of gasoline. To contain emissions from the road sector, and in particular the emissions of heavy transport – which is usually a heavy diesel user – Costa Rica could increase the tax rate on diesel at least to the level of the tax rate on gasoline.

In Costa Rica, the effective tax rates on carbon emissions from fuels used for heating and process purposes and electricity generation do not consistently reflect the external costs of carbon emissions. In general, ensuring that a uniform carbon price covers as many emissions as possible maximises the cost-effectiveness of abating emissions and prevents future emissions growth. In Costa Rica, the mix of fuels used for residential heating, industry and the public and commercial sector (presented in Figure 5.2 as "heating and process use"), is very diverse and consists of a range of oil products, coal, natural gas, biomass, waste and renewables. Of these, all oil products (LPG, fuel oil and diesel) are taxed although at lower rates on average than gasoline and diesel, which are predominantly used in the transport sector. This is usual practice in most countries, since – in the absence of more targeted policy instruments – taxes on transport fuels are commonly thought of as also addressing other (non-carbon) external costs from the road transport sector (see Table 5.1).

Figure 5.2. **Effective tax rates on energy use in Costa Rica, in terms of carbon content**

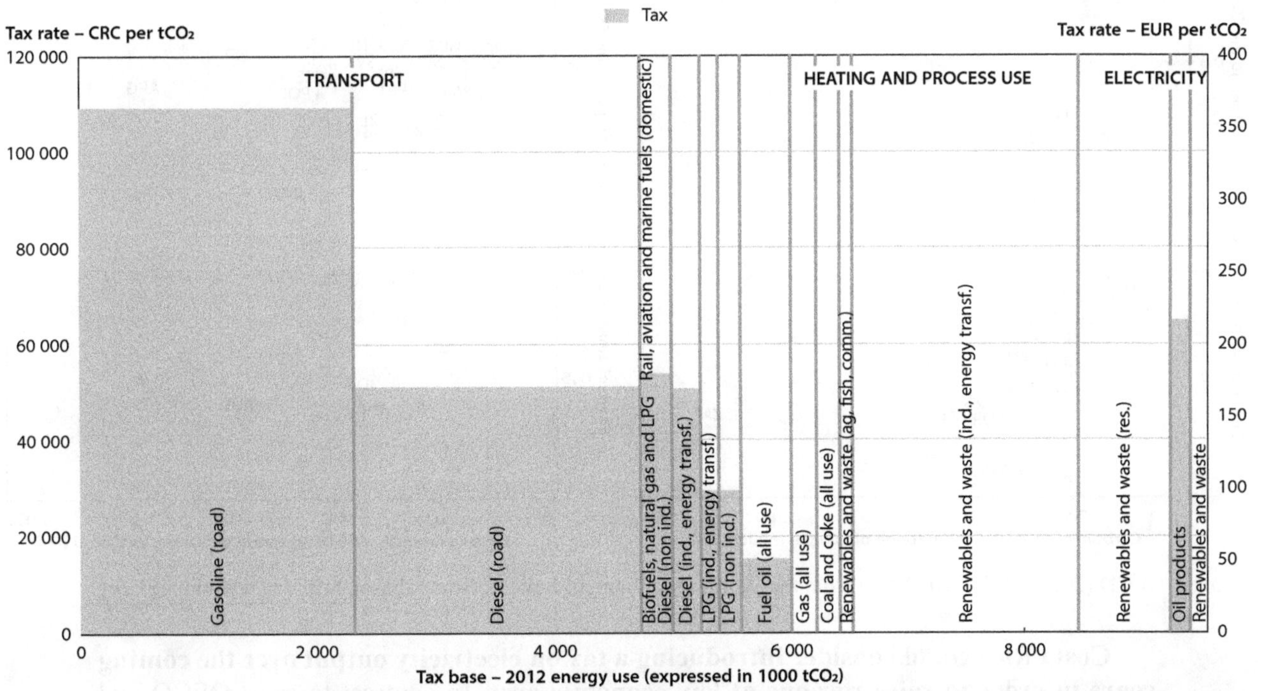

Source: OECD calculations. Tax rates are as of 1 April 2017; energy use data is for 2012 from IEA (2014), "Extended world energy balances", *IEA World Energy Statistics and Balances* (database), http://dx.doi.org/10.1787/data-00513-en.

The external cost of combusting other fossil fuels, such as coal, is entirely unpriced. While coal currently accounts for a small share of total carbon emissions from energy use in Costa Rica (around 2%), extending a tax to all fossil fuels (including coal and natural gas) could help prevent future increases in their use in industry, by households and for electricity generation. This would reduce the likelihood that these fossil fuels would replace electricity generation from hydro in the future (i.e. in case the use of hydro decreases further as a result of climatic change). As mentioned earlier, electricity production currently produces almost no carbon emissions in Costa Rica. Within the fossil fuels used to produce electricity, oil products dominate, and are priced at the same rates as the fuels used for heating and process purposes. Pricing all fuels, including those used in electricity generation, at rates that reflect their carbon content (so, at the very least at EUR 30 per tCO_2, and, where possible, also of other GHG emitted on combustion) would ensure that energy users consider the external costs of combusting fuel in their usage decisions, and prevent future emissions increases.

Countries that price larger shares of carbon emissions also have a lower carbon-intensity of GDP. Analysis included in OECD (2015a) and (OECD, 2016b) shows that most countries do not consistently price carbon emissions from energy use at rates that reflect the carbon content of fuels. However, Figure 5.3 suggests that countries which price a larger share of carbon emissions from energy use tend to have a lower carbon-intensity of GDP. In view of Costa Rica's target to achieve carbon-neutrality by 2021, it could thus be considered to work towards enlarging the share of carbon emissions which are taxed, and pricing them in line with the carbon content of fuels.

Figure 5.3. **Proportion of CO_2 emissions priced above EUR 30 (left) and EUR 0 (right) per tonne of CO_2 relative to the carbon intensity of GDP, 41 countries, 2012**

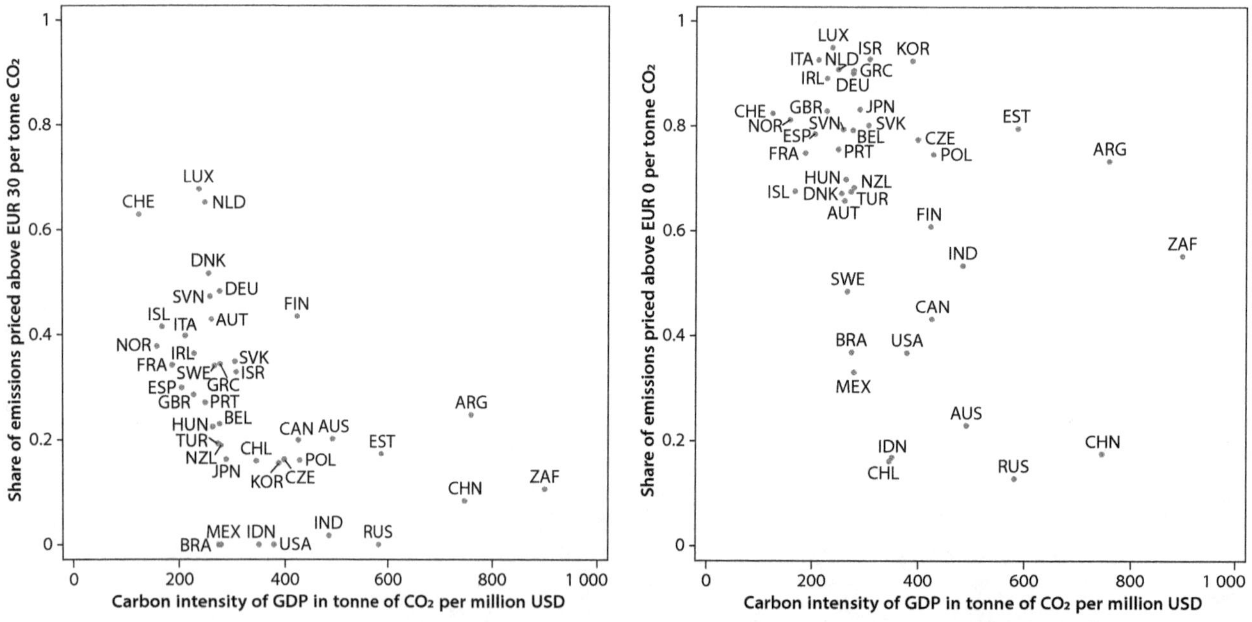

Source: OECD (2016b), using GDP data from the World Development Indicators (database), http://data.worldbank.org/.

Costa Rica could consider introducing a tax on electricity output over the coming years in order to raise revenue at low economic cost. In contrast to most OECD and G20 economies, Costa Rica does not levy a tax on electricity output. Taxes on electricity can be efficient revenue-raising instruments, because the demand for electricity is not very price-elastic. In addition, taxes on electricity tend to be more difficult to avoid than direct taxes, such as CIT, since they are usually included in the price of electricity and are thus paid directly with the electricity bill. There is widespread concern that lower income households would be hit particularly hard by taxes on electricity output. There are, however, effective and proven ways to compensate for any potential regressive effects of electricity taxes. Policy makers can, for example, provide targeted compensation payments to poor households (e.g. using income-tested compensation or lump sum transfers). An alternative way to address distributional concerns would be to exempt small amounts of electricity consumption from taxation. To facilitate adjustment for electricity users, rates could be introduced at low rates, and gradually increased over time.

A tax on electricity output should go hand in hand with taxing fossil fuel inputs to electricity generation under a fuel tax, with rates aligned with the carbon content and the broader pollution profile of the respective fossil fuel, as described in the preceding paragraphs. This is because, if the fuel mix is not fixed, then taxes on input fuels and taxes on electricity use affect different behavioural margins. For example, a tax on electricity use does not steer fuel mixes in a particular direction (low carbon), whereas taxes on input fuels do have that potential. Although the fuel mix to generate electricity in Costa Rica is currently low-carbon, levying a tax on fuel inputs to electricity can help preventing increases in the carbon intensity of the electricity generation mix in the future.

Fuels subject to the fuel tax are exempt from all taxes on imports, including the sales tax, which translates into a *de facto* preferential tax treatment of energy products. As discussed earlier in this chapter, fuel taxes are an appropriate way to have consumers factor the external costs of fuel use into their consumption choices. Other taxes, such as import duties, VAT or sales taxes also increase the prices of energy products, but these taxes are usually not specific to energy products. Thus, they do not change the relative price level of energy products versus other goods and services. However, if the rates of these taxes are differentiated in such a way that they strongly affect the relative price of energy products, they become *de facto* specific to such products. In Costa Rica, fuels subject to the fuel tax are exempt from all sales taxes. Reducing these sales taxes selectively for energy products counteracts the intention to increase the relative end-user prices of energy (for environmental and revenue-raising reasons). This effect is particularly pronounced if the differential rates apply only to energy products, as is the case in Costa Rica. To counteract this effect, it could be considered to also levy VAT and import duties on the goods subject to the fuel tax (see chapter 4). Any attempts to reflect the external costs of fuel use, and differentiate the prices of energy products via à vis other goods should be implemented via excise taxes, and not via sales taxes, VAT or taxes on import, which should ideally apply to the broadest possible range of goods and services.

There is scope to adapt the taxation of motor vehicles to reflect the external costs of vehicle use more closely

Costa Rica taxes the ownership and purchase of vehicles via different instruments. Vehicle ownership is taxed on an annual basis, at differential rates according to vehicle type and use (Table 5.2). While private vehicles are taxed at rates that increase with the price of the vehicle, motorcycles are taxed according to engine displacement. Taxis, buses and trucks pay a flat rate under the ownership tax, at roughly a third of the minimum tax for private cars. With regard to vehicle purchases, two taxes apply. The selective consumption tax levies *ad valorem* rates on the cost, insurance and freight (CIF) value of vehicles. The tax also applies to domestic car purchases, but, due to the absence of a domestic car industry, the tax falls on vehicle imports only. Higher differential rates are levied on vehicles older than seven years, lower rates on hybrid vehicles, and electric cars are zero-rated. The sales tax (13%) and a tax based on Law 6946 (1%) apply on top of these taxes, but their rates do not vary by type of vehicle or the type of fuel used. Since, in most countries, value-added and sales taxes do not introduce *de facto* specific variation in the relative prices of different products, these taxes are not counted as specific taxes on vehicle use, and are also not included in Table 5.2.[2]

Table 5.2. **Specific taxes levied on motor vehicles in Costa Rica, as in 2016**

		Import or purchase		Domestic re-sale	Ownership
		Import duty	Selected consumption tax	Tax on the sale of used vehicles	Annual tax on the ownership of motor vehicles
Fuel type	Vehicle type	Sales price			
100% fossil	Private passenger cars (new, <7 years)	0%	30%	2.5%	Increasing with vehicle value
	Private passenger cars (>7 years)	0%	48%		
	Buses	5%	23%-43%		Flat at CRC 80 000
	Taxis	0%	30%		
	Trucks	14%	14%-48%		
Hybrid	All vehicles, new	0%	10%		Like other private passenger cars vehicles (see above)
Electric	All vehicles, new	0%	0%		

Note: The sales tax (13%) and a tax based on Law 6946 (1%) apply in addition to the taxes included in this table, but these two taxes do not vary by type of vehicle or the type of fuel used.

Source: Collected from laws and regulations.

The design of these taxes could be adapted to encourage purchasing less-polluting vehicles. While the tax rates differentiate by vehicle age and type to some extent, there is scope to tailor them more closely to the external costs of road use. The existing taxes on vehicle ownership and transfer could be supplemented with rate components based on the average emissions of the car in grams per kilometre, to encourage consumers to shift towards less polluting cars, as was done in Chile (Box 5.3). Moreover, the flat rates paid by buses, taxis and trucks under the tax on vehicle ownership could be reconsidered, and would ideally map to the rates paid by other vehicles. This would extend the incentives to move towards less polluting cars to these user groups. Furthermore, it could be useful to analyse whether the tax on the sale of used vehicles provides adequate incentive to renew the vehicle fleet.

To raise revenues, the design of vehicle taxes should nevertheless remain simple. Achieving a well-targeted vehicle tax that raises revenues while also reducing transport emissions is difficult. For example, the French experience with the "bonus-malus" system – a vehicle sales tax varying in line with the cars' carbon emissions – has shown that a too granular variation in vehicle taxes by the vehicle's environmental impact risks unnecessarily foregoing revenues, with uncertain additional impacts on emissions (d'Haultfoeuille et al., 2014).[3] In contrast, the government of Israel introduced a purchase tax on vehicles, which has been very effective at influencing purchase behaviour and reducing the emissions of the vehicle fleet, but tax revenues have quickly eroded after the introduction of this tax (Roshal and Tovias, 2016). In many cases, a fuel tax that differentiates between the carbon content of different fuels, as described above, can achieve emissions reductions at a lower cost than a very differentiated vehicle tax. Consequently, in Costa Rica, maintaining a vehicle tax rate component based on the price of the vehicle, motor size, or similar, together with some differentiation by environmental criteria could strike a balance between revenue-raising and environmental objectives.

Box 5.3. **Examples from Chile: Vehicle taxation and road pricing**

A number of OECD member countries apply vehicle taxes that vary with the fuel efficiency or CO_2 emissions of the vehicles; fewer countries address local air pollutants in their vehicle taxes (Israel and Norway are among the exceptions). Since January 2015, Chile has been phasing in a tax on new private passenger vehicle registrations. Such a tax can help gradually modify the composition of the car fleet. From an environmental point of view, however, it is less efficient than taxes on vehicle fuels and road pricing because it is not linked to vehicle use.

The Chilean tax is differentiated according to the vehicles' test-cycle urban fuel efficiency, their NO_X emissions, and their retail price. The government has been phasing in the NO_X element of the tax gradually; with the full value applied from 2017. Since the tax has been applied only for a short period, it is not yet possible to assess its overall impact. Some indications, however, suggest that consumption is changing in the expected directions, with increasing market share for low-emission vehicles. Analysis included in OECD and ECLAC (2016) illustrates how the tax varies depending on the NO_X emissions for different levels of fuel efficiency. It uses a passenger vehicle with an assumed retail price of approximately USD 10 000 as the example. The tax in per cent of the retail price increases proportionally with NO_X emissions. At the Euro-5 NO_X emission limit for diesel vehicles, the tax rate is 8% to 9% of the retail price, given the selected fuel efficiency levels. For a petrol vehicle complying with the Euro-5 limit, the tax rate is 3% to 4% (the Euro-5 emission limit is stricter for petrol vehicles than for diesel vehicles). Accordingly, in absolute terms, the petrol vehicle would pay in the order of USD 500 less in tax than the diesel one, in line with the higher NO_X emissions from diesel use, compared to petrol.

Figure 5.4. **The Chilean vehicle tax is lower for cleaner and cheaper vehicles**

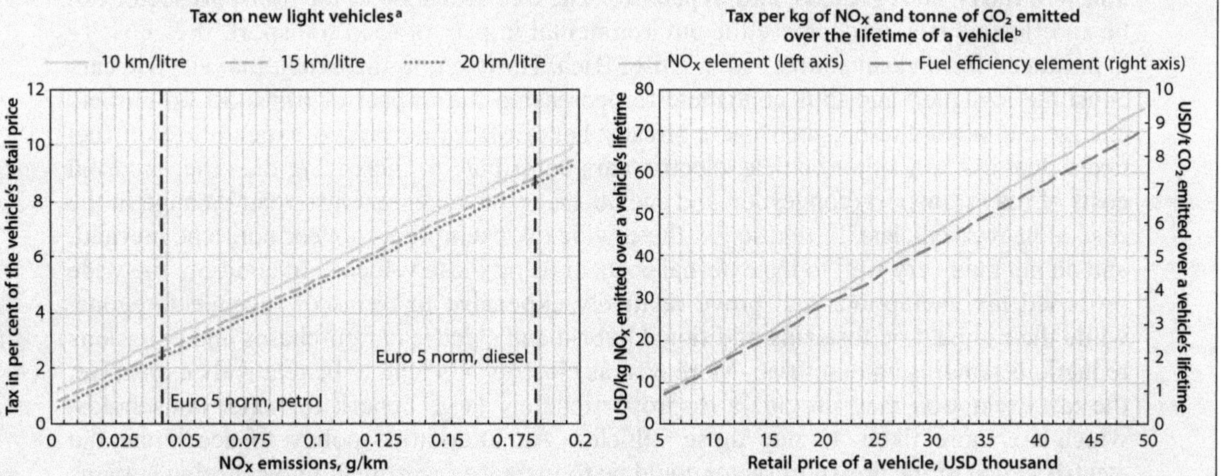

StatLink http://dx.doi.org/10.1787/888933545120

Notes: a. The tax level depends on the price of the vehicles. In this chart, data refer to vehicles with an assumed retail price of CLP 6 000 000 (approximately USD 9 000). The tax rates shown are for 2017.

b. The calculation assumes that each vehicle is driven 200 000 km over its lifetime. The tax rates shown are for 2017.

Source: OECD/ECLAC (2016).

Box 5.3. **Examples from Chile: Vehicle taxation and road pricing** *(continued)*

Toll road concessions, which Chile has been granting to private operators since the 1990s, helped significantly expand the country's highway network, including around the Santiago Metropolitan Region. Santiago was the world's first city to implement urban highways almost simultaneously with interoperable free-flow toll charges.[1] Tolls reflect both the cost of road use and externalities linked to traffic, namely congestion. They increase with the length of road stretches and weight of vehicles, and vary with time of day (off-peak, peak or saturation).[2] Congestion charges have economic and environmental advantages. They allow not only for recovery of investment costs, but also for adequate pricing of limited space, environmental externalities (e.g. air pollution) and fairer competition among different transport modes. Linking the tolls to emission levels and fuel efficiency of vehicles would further stimulate a shift towards cleaner vehicles.

Notes: 1. Highways were tendered to different operators. An inter-operable free-flow tele-toll allows users to avoid stopping when paying the toll, passing under a portico that permits information to be exchanged for automatic invoicing.

2. Peak time rates come into effect when traffic reduces the average travelling speed to levels below the road's design speed; saturation rates come into effect when average speeds are far below the level designed for the road.

Source: OECD/ECLAC (2016).

Costa Rica is discussing new policies to stimulate the electrification of the transport sector. Current plans include exempting all electric vehicles and their spare parts, from all import tariffs, the selective consumption and the sales tax, the restrictions on vehicle circulation in the San José Metropolitan Area and all parking fees. These exemptions will apply irrespective of the vehicle's value, size and type, though a maximum exemption is discussed, based on vehicle price. In addition, the purchase of electric vehicles would be partially deductible from the income tax. These policies would be valid for 5 years, or until the number of electric vehicles in Costa Rica arrives at 100 000.

The proposed tax exemptions for electric vehicles appear not very well targeted, and will likely be regressive and expensive. The electrification of the transport sector can be an effective way to decrease the environmental impact of road transport, if electricity is produced from clean sources as in Costa Rica. However, to the extent that electric cars consume less fuel, and thus contribute to decreasing the impact of transport on climate change and air pollution, their users already benefit from decreased expenditure on fuel taxes. Just like any other vehicle, electric cars contribute to increasing the other external costs of road transport (congestion and accidents, and to an extent also road damage in the case of heavy vehicles). In that sense, these wide tax exemptions appear not to be merited, and do not map very well to the external costs of using these vehicles. In addition, the wide proposed tax exemptions can prove relatively expensive in terms of revenue foregone, while their impact on fostering additional hybrid and electric car purchases and emissions reductions remains unquantified. Moreover, as electric cars tend to be relatively expensive, the tax exemption may provide a disproportionately large benefit to richer households, which are more likely to buy those vehicles. An alternative policy to accelerate the electrification of the transport sector could be to increase investment into charging stations and other necessary infrastructure for electrification. For the same reasons, the zero-rating of electric vehicles and the reduced rate for hybrid cars under the selective consumption tax could be reconsidered as well.

Costa Rica could consider moving away from driving restrictions in the capital area, and extending price-based measures

Despite driving restrictions in the San José Metropolitan Area, congestion and air pollution remain high. To regulate traffic and congestion, private cars are banned from the San José Greater Metropolitan area on one day per week, depending on the last digit of their license plate. Exemptions exist for motorcycles, public transport and taxis, rental cars, or for vehicles carrying five or more persons in peak hours. However, though the driving restrictions have been in place largely uninterrupted since August 2005, congestion and air pollution around the capital are large.

There is evidence that driving restrictions are a relatively expensive policy. While driving restrictions encourage reduced driving (e.g. through encouraging alternate travel modes, and pointed reductions of travel on the specific days the drivers' car is concerned), they do not allow drivers to adapt in all possible ways (e.g. avoiding trips during rush hours). As a result, the welfare cost associated with driving restrictions can be high. Furthermore, evidence from similar policies (e.g. in Mexico City) shows that richer drivers respond to driving restrictions by purchasing additional cars, which tend to be older and more polluting (Davis, 2008). In consequence, Costa Rica could consider gradually moving away from driving restrictions towards more price-based measures, such as making parking in the city centre more expensive. In the mid- to longer run, it could be considered to move towards cordon fees, as was done in Santiago de Chile (Box 5.3), Singapore, London and Stockholm.

There is scope to increase the neutrality of the taxation of electricity producers and electricity use

To level the playing field for electricity producers, it could be considered to align the tax treatment of private and municipal electricity producers. While public entities, such as the national electricity producer ICE (which controls 74.1% of generation capacity), and all private electricity producers (7.2% of generation capacity) are subject to CIT, municipal electricity producers (11.01% of generation capacity), are exempt from CIT. The differential tax treatment of electricity producers appears to create a competitive advantage for municipal electricity producers, with no apparent underlying economic rationale.[4]

The wide range of tax exemptions provided for energy-efficient goods are a relatively expensive policy to encourage their use. A range of goods which are deemed as energy efficient or low-carbon is exempt from import taxes (i.e. from the selective consumption tax and the sales tax). This policy does not appear to be cost-effective in reducing emissions. While, in principle, tax incentives or other subsidies do modify relative prices of environmental goods just like carbon prices do, they have a number of important limitations. For example, tax subsidies inevitably involve "picking winners", and tax incentives are frequently found to subsidise actions that would have been taken in their absence, while resulting in limited additional carbon abatement (see Greene and Braathen, 2014, for a more detailed discussion). As a result, approaches that tax energy-inefficient goods rather than subsidise energy-efficient goods are preferred. Well-designed carbon prices and, possibly, incentives for better insulation of buildings, are alternative and cheaper ways to foster energy efficiency and low carbon production of electricity.

The proposed tax on non-recyclable plastic containers can be an effective way to reduce their use

Costa Rica is considering the introduction of a specific tax on non-recyclable plastic containers. In other countries, low tax rates on non-reusable waste, such as the tax on plastic bags levied in the UK and Ireland, have been shown to be very effective at reducing waste from these products. For example, in the United Kingdom, a small charge on plastic bags has decreased the use of plastic bags by 6 billion in the first months of 2016, compared to the previous year (Barkham, 2016). The environmental effects of such a tax can be large, though, due to the potentially large elasticity of the tax base and the low rate, public revenues from this tax are likely to be relatively modest.

There is opportunity to increase the cost-efficiency of the Payments for Environmental Services Programme

Costa Rica operates a broad and well-known Payments for Environmental Services Programme. Through the Payments for Environmental Services Programme (PSA, by its acronym in Spanish), operated by the designated National Fund for Forest Financing (FONAFIFO), the government contracts forest owners for the services provided by their land and prevent deforestation. Four environmental services are recognised by the Costa Rican government, which are assumed to be equally provided by each hectare of forest; mitigation of greenhouse gas emissions, water protection, conservation of biodiversity and landscape beauty.

The PSA Programme overlaps with a range of competing regulations, and the direct impacts of the programme could be quantified better. The PSA is cited as a large success in reversing deforestation in Costa Rica. Over half of the country's territory is now covered by forests, compared to just 26% in 1983 (World Bank, 2016). The programme overlaps with a range of other policies, such as a ban on land-use change and a law promoting the recovery of secondary forests (IIED, 2013). As a result, it is difficult to trace back which part of environmental benefits results from the PSA, or other policies. To increase the cost effectiveness of the programme in delivering environmental services, it could be considered to conduct a cost-benefit analysis of the policy.

The levels of PSA payments could be aligned more closely with the likelihood of deforestation of a given hectare. Forest owners are paid a lump sum per hectare of forest conserved, at levels fixed each year by the government. However, applications by farmers for participating in the programme consistently exceed available funding. Further decreases in the level may make certain parts of the land more amenable to land use change, in particular when the opportunity cost of the land is high. A potential way forward would be to align the amount of payments per hectare more closely with the opportunity cost of the land use. For example, payments could be varied in line to their distance from a city, and other indicators determining land value. This is would be in line with recent efforts to move away from the first-come, first-serve basis of awarding PSA contracts, towards prioritising areas more critical to conservation. Furthermore, it could be considered to de-link the funding of the programme from fluctuations in fuel tax revenues.

The tax policy recommendations that can be drawn from this analysis are as follows:

Recommendations

- Align the rates of the fuel tax with the carbon content of the underlying fuels. This includes increasing the tax rate on diesel at least to the level of the tax on gasoline, and introducing tax rates on coal and natural gas.
- Phase out the import and sales tax exemptions for fuels.
- Introduce over time a tax on electricity output to foster a more efficient use of electricity, while addressing the distributional effects of such a tax.
- Adapt the vehicle taxes to better address pollution and congestion, for example by supplementing the vehicle taxes by a rate on pollution (e.g. NO_X emissions).
- Align the taxation of taxis, trucks and buses with that of other vehicles.
- Replace the proposed broad tax exemptions for electric cars with increased investment into transport infrastructure, including the infrastructure necessary to use electric cars.
- Align the taxation of municipal and private electricity producers.
- Evaluate the tax exemptions for energy-efficient products with regards to their cost-effectiveness in achieving emissions reductions.
- Evaluate the additionality of the PSA programme in providing environmental services.

Notes

1. The manufacturing and energy production industry, the residential and commercial sector, and the agriculture sector accounted for 23.9%, 1.7%, and 4.5% of emissions, respectively, in 2012. Note that the estimates of the shares of GHG emissions by sector vary, depending on the method used to account for emissions from biomass. While the United Nations Framework Commission for Climate Change (UNFCCC) generally takes a lifecycle approach to accounting for the emissions from biomass (and counts them as zero), OECD (2015 and 2016) does not zero-rate emissions from the combustion of biomass. The figures shown in this chapter are aligned with the approach taken in OECD (2015) and OECD (2016).
2. Domestic transactions involving used vehicles are taxed at 2.5% of the sales price, with no differentiation by vehicle or motor type.
3. An evaluation of the French policy has shown that granting overly generous reductions in vehicle taxes can be counterproductive, by increasing automobile sales and carbon emissions compared to the baseline. Braathen (2009, 2011) shows that CO_2 abatement achieved through differentiated vehicle taxes can be relatively costly.
4. OECD (2016c) discusses the way electricity tariffs are set in Costa Rica, and compares them to the tariff-setting methodology in selected OECD countries. The key take-away of that discussion is that the way electricity tariffs are set by the Public Services Regulatory Authority (*Autoridad Reguladora de las Servicio Públicos*, ARESEP) does not provide strong incentives for cost reductions by electricity producers.

References

Climate Action Tracker (2015), *Costa Rica*, http://climateactiontracker.org/countries/costarica.html.

Barkham, P. (2016), "Six billion plastic bags can't be wrong – so what do we tax next?", *The Guardian*, 3 October 2016, https://www.theguardian.com/environment/shortcuts/2016/oct/03/six-billion-plastic-bags-cant-be-wrong-so-what-do-we-tax-next.

Braathen, N. A. (2011), "Carbon-related taxation in OECD countries and interactions between policy instruments", in Larry Kreiser, Julsuchada Sirisom, Hope Ashiabor and Janet Milne (eds.), *Environmental Taxation and Climate Change: Achieving Environmental Sustainability through Fiscal Policy, Critical Issues in Environmental Taxation*, Volume X, Edward Elgar, p.3-19.

Braathen, N. A. (2009), "Incentives for CO_2 emission reductions in current motor vehicle taxes", Paper prepared for the OECD Working Party on National Environmental Policies, www.oecd.org/officialdocuments/publicdisplaydocumentpdf/?cote=env/epoc/wpnep/t(2009)2/final&doclanguage=en.

IIED (2013), *Learning From 20 Years of Payments for Ecosystem Services in Costa Rica*, http://pubs.iied.org/16514IIED/.

Harding, M. (2014), "The diesel differential: differences in the tax treatment of gasoline and diesel for road use", *OECD Taxation Working Papers*, No. 21, OECD Publishing, Paris, http://dx.doi.org/10.1787/5jz14cd7hk6b-en.

Davis, L.W (2008), "The effect of driving restrictions on air quality in Mexico City", *Journal of Political Economy*, 116: 38-81.

Granoff et al. (2015), "Bridging Costa Rica's green growth gap", *ODI Research Reports and Studies*, https://www.odi.org/publications/9865-bridging-costa-ricas-green-growth-gap-support-further-transformation-toward-green-economy.

Greene, J. and N. Braathen (2014), "Tax Preferences for Environmental Goals: Use, Limitations and Preferred Practices", *OECD Environment Working Papers*, No. 71, OECD Publishing, Paris, http://dx.doi.org/10.1787/5jxwrr4hkd6l-en.

MINAE – Ministry of Environment Costa Rica (2015a), *Intended Nationally Determined Contribution*, http://www4.unfccc.int/submissions/INDC/Published%20Documents/Costa%20Rica/1/INDC%20Costa%20Rica%20Version%202%200%20final%20ENG.pdf.

MINAE – Ministry of Environment Costa Rica (2015b), *Informe Bienal de Actualización ante la Convención Marco de las Naciones Unidas sobre el Cambio Climático* [Bi-annual update report to the United Nations framework convention on Climate Change], http://unfccc.int/resource/docs/natc/corbur1.pdf.

MINAE – Ministry of Environment Costa Rica (2014), *Plan Nacional de Energía 2015-2030* [National Energy Plan 2015-2030], www.minae.go.cr/recursos/2015/pdf/VII-PNE.pdf.

OECD (2016a), *The Economic Consequences of Outdoor Air Pollution*, OECD Publishing, Paris, http://dx.doi.org/10.1787/9789264257474-en.

OECD (2016b), *Effective Carbon Rates: Pricing CO2 Through Taxes and Emissions Trading Systems*, OECD Publishing, Paris, http://dx.doi.org/10.1787/9789264260115-en.

OECD (2016c), *OECD Economic Surveys: Costa Rica 2016: Economic Assessment*, OECD Publishing, Paris, http://dx.doi.org/10.1787/eco_surveys-cri-2016-en.

OECD (2015a), *Taxing Energy Use 2015: OECD and Selected Partner Economies*, OECD Publishing, Paris, http://dx.doi.org/10.1787/9789264232334-en.

OECD (2015b), *Aligning Policies for a Low-Carbon Economy*, OECD Publishing, Paris, http://dx.doi.org/10.1787/9789264233294-en.

OECD (2013a), *Effective Carbon Prices*, OECD Publishing, Paris, http://dx.doi.org/10.1787/9789264196964-en.

OECD (2013b), *Taxing Energy Use: A Graphical Analysis*, OECD Publishing, Paris, http://dx.doi.org/10.1787/9789264183933-en.

OECD/ECLAC (2016), *OECD Environmental Performance Reviews: Chile 2016*, OECD Publishing, Paris, http://dx.doi.org/10.1787/9789264252615-en.

Van Dender, K., I. Parry (forthcoming), "Taxing vehicles, fuel, and use: what tax mix for road transport?", OECD Discussion Paper.

WHO (2016), *Ambient Air Pollution: A Global Assessment of Exposure and Burden of Disease*, World Health Organization, Geneva, www.who.int/phe/publications/air-pollution-global-assessment/en/.

World Bank (2016), *Accounting Reveals that Costa Rica's Forest Wealth is Greater Than Expected*, www.worldbank.org/en/news/feature/2016/05/31/accounting-reveals-that-costa-ricas-forest-wealth-is-greater-than-expected.

ORGANISATION FOR ECONOMIC CO-OPERATION AND DEVELOPMENT

The OECD is a unique forum where governments work together to address the economic, social and environmental challenges of globalisation. The OECD is also at the forefront of efforts to understand and to help governments respond to new developments and concerns, such as corporate governance, the information economy and the challenges of an ageing population. The Organisation provides a setting where governments can compare policy experiences, seek answers to common problems, identify good practice and work to co-ordinate domestic and international policies.

The OECD member countries are: Australia, Austria, Belgium, Canada, Chile, the Czech Republic, Denmark, Estonia, Finland, France, Germany, Greece, Hungary, Iceland, Ireland, Israel, Italy, Japan, Korea, Latvia, Luxembourg, Mexico, the Netherlands, New Zealand, Norway, Poland, Portugal, the Slovak Republic, Slovenia, Spain, Sweden, Switzerland, Turkey, the United Kingdom and the United States. The European Union takes part in the work of the OECD.

OECD Publishing disseminates widely the results of the Organisation's statistics gathering and research on economic, social and environmental issues, as well as the conventions, guidelines and standards agreed by its members.

OECD PUBLISHING, 2, rue André-Pascal, 75775 PARIS CEDEX 16
(23 2017 06 1 P) ISBN 978-92-64-27770-0 – 2017

www.ingramcontent.com/pod-product-compliance
Lightning Source LLC
Chambersburg PA
CBHW061222240926
51846CB00006B/1312